Fanatical at Liberty Praise for John Hewitt

"John looks at what people can become, not what they are now."
- *Sandy Raiter/Tax Specialist*

"John Hewitt has also been a positive influence in my life. Our CEO walks around in shorts and tee shirts. He really does have an open door policy. One day, I walked in to his office and asked him to buy Girl Scout cookies. He bought a box of each!"
- *Patricia Old/Area Development Assistant*

"When it's all said and done, the opportunities created by Liberty, by John Hewitt, have forever changed my life… I have found value in my intelligence, my creativity, and myself. I know my worth and I have John to thank for that."
- *Heather Smith/Corporate Director and Franchisee Family*

"While Liberty is on the path to be the top tax service by 2020, John and the rest of the Liberty family stay true to the professed top values of God, family, and business."
- *Dennis Dercks/Area Developer - WI*

"John Hewitt looks out and sees people willing to work hard and follow the Liberty motto of: Set the Standard, Improve Each Day and Have Some Fun."
- *Todd & Karen Swicegood/Franchisees – NC*

"John Hewitt has had a huge influence on my life. John's advice (is) "First things first, second things - not at all." I truly believed, and still believe, that John would make a success of any venture in which he invested his time, energy, and leadership capabilities."
- *Kathleen Curry/Corporate Counsel*

"Everybody dreams, but I didn't know if it was possible. The system that John Hewitt has put in place made the difference. He tells you what needs to be done and when it needs to be done. Timing is very important – if you do things at the right time, then you become successful."
- *Bablu Shahabuddin/Franchisee and Area Developer*

"John Hewitt is a person of integrity: giving and forgiving."
- *Margaret Taylor/Franchisee - Virginia Beach, VA*

"One thing I have learned is that when John suggests a new venture, he has put a lot of thought into his recommendation. It gives us great pride to help (franchisees) achieve business and life goals and dreams, and this experience would never have been possible without the support of John Hewitt."
- *Nancy Nelson/ Executive Assistant and Area Developer*

"I learned more from John about business management, people management and human relations than I ever did in MBA school and in my Fortune 50 corporate career… John is all about helping other people. One thing about John's desire to help others that really stands out to me is his passion to stop world hunger."
- *Jack Seal/Franchisee and Former VP of Finance*

"The reason I invested with John is that I knew he was totally honest. It's important to know that one thing you don't have to worry about is whether the owner is trying to do his best for the company and the stockholders. No matter how good your plans may be, they can go wrong. That's an unavoidable risk, but it's compounded if you can't be sure of the integrity of the owner. With John, this was never an issue."
- *Jim Davis/Liberty Tax Investor*

"I've had a lot of support from all the good people at Liberty and John Hewitt himself. I owe a lot to this company, and I am extremely loyal as a result of the opportunity they have given me. What other company would give me a chance to be in business for myself at 19 years old?"
- *Jesus Rivas/Franchisee – Allentown, PA*

"I followed John to LIBERTY in 2005, and continued to learn and to break new boundaries. I feel that God provided the perseverance, which was the key ingredient to achieving my goals. I am thankful for that and He used John to open a door."
- *Diane Wagner/ Area Developer, RI*

"John took a chance on me. Liberty has changed my life forever!"
- *Nancy Simonsen/Corporate Office Manager*

"I had no idea how to manage or own a business. It happened because a man named John Hewitt believed in me much more than I ever believed in myself. He gave me the opportunity to prove it and to change my life forever. Every step of the journey, through the highs and lows, the good and the bad, he was always there for me and I will be eternally grateful."
- *Sue Wickham/National Site Selection Director*

"My parent's strong belief in John Hewitt and Liberty fueled my sales success… No amount of money can match how much John and Liberty have changed my life. When I first arrived at Liberty, I didn't know what the heck I was doing. I didn't even understand what a franchise was. I never dreamed this would be my life now. You don't have to be a rocket scientist; you just need the desire to succeed. My life – our daughter's life – will never be the same."
- *Sandy Stow/VP of Area Development*

"John is a brilliant strategist and hopes to use his business experience and success to create a sustainable model to end hunger around the globe."
- *Carolyn Castleberry/Director of Special Projects*

iCOMPETE

My Extraordinary
Strategy for Winning

By John T. Hewitt

aBM

Published by:
A Book's Mind
PO Box 272847
Fort Collins, CO 80527

The information in this book is not intended to serve as legal advice related to individual situations. The author has taken reasonable precautions in preparing text and believes the facts presented here are accurate as of the date the book was written. Neither the author nor the publisher assume any responsibility for errors or omissions, and the author and publisher specifically disclaim any liability resulting from the use or application of the information contained in this book.

For information:
JTH Publishing, LLC
1716 Corporate Landing Parkway
Virginia Beach, VA 23454
www.libertytax.com

About John and Liberty Tax Service

Liberty Tax Service Founder and CEO, John Hewitt, is fanatical about taxes and unmatched customer service. A nationally recognized name in the tax return preparation and accounting world, Hewitt is a veteran of 46 tax seasons, the founder of two top tax preparation firms, and a former H&R Block Regional Director. *Accounting Today* magazine has named Hewitt one of the accounting profession's Top 100 most influential people fifteen times. The International Franchise Association honored Hewitt as its Entrepreneur of the Year in February 2006.

One of the things that makes Liberty Tax unique is how supportive we are of our franchisees and their fanatical commitment to change the world. Culture defines Liberty and it's time for the world to know the stories of our owners, employees, partners, clients, and friends. Our tax return preparation franchise has consistently been recognized as a leader among all franchises, not just personal income tax based businesses. We have been awarded a top spot among franchises by magazines such as *Black Enterprise, Poder/Hispanic Enterprise*, and *Military Times Edge*. *Accounting Today* named Liberty Tax to its "Top Tax Firms" list from 2010 through 2014. Liberty Tax Service has been ranked as one of the top franchise opportunities on *Entrepreneur* magazine's annual Franchise 500 every year from 1998 to 2014.

As of this writing, there are more than 4,400 Liberty Tax Service offices operating in the United States and Canada, where we operate as Liberty Tax Service Canada. Liberty Tax Service started in Canada on September 1, 1997 when John acquired a Canadian tax franchisor, U&R Tax Depot. In 1998, we became Liberty Tax Service and opened five offices in the United States. Our goal is to become the #1 tax service in the universe by 2020. Culture and giving back drive that vision.

Dedication

One of my core beliefs is that you can never give more than you receive in life. Because of my competitive nature, I have a fanatical goal to give to every human being more than they give me, knowing that the only two people you can never catch are your parents - if you have great parents - and I do.

This book is dedicated to my mom and dad who gave me more than I can ever repay.

Contents

Foreword by Gordon D'Angelo
Live, Listen, Learn

John Hewitt has been a life changer for a multitude of people, producing a positive effect. He portrays confidence and delivers results. He exchanges optimism after listening through your extensive concerns. He inserts realistic dosages of inspiration at a higher level than you originally thought possible and exhibits a dedicated, loyal characteristic of no turning back. Obstacles do not prevent him from success. This prompts you to focus and take bold steps to overcome your perceived adversity on route to your intended promised land.

John loves to encourage others. Wisely, he challenges what you are saying or presenting, giving you the opportunity to find and deliver reality. This directly increases your capacity and arms you with a stronger sense of preparation for future proposals. His higher viewpoint usually makes most people's maximum his minimum. In addition, he provides resources, support, and consistency in making himself available. He projects intellectual and material tangibility to a project, which brings a spirit of freedom and a strong energy to proceed.

During any discussion with John, debating, disappointment, decisions, and discovery are likely to make an appearance. You can fret or whine, get mad or learn, but note his intention is for you to grow. Like others, his world can get congested because of size and dimension. Yet he will find time for you. I've been there fighting and observing through the great and disastrous times. Yet the only outcome he ever speaks about is winning.

Gratitude is not his reward or motivation, nor is recognition. Thank God. Surely he's been shorted. I feel his fulfillment comes from attaining a predetermined vision. Thousands, and even extended generations to come, have benefited from his ability to the stay the course.

Though I've had many successes in my life, without a doubt, John has been my number one human resource. Much of my hybrid operating fuel was ignited through conversations with John and witnessing his pathways. I've listened intently and taken countless pages of notes and, yes, it has paid off. One ounce of his commentary can lead to tons of growth. The value of his willingness to relate to others is immeasurable. He has perpetuated amazing

outcomes from every level of the situational scoreboard. Sharing any experience with John through speaking, writing, or listening should be treated as a learning opportunity and respected as a gift for those who wish to achieve their own success.

- **Gordon D'Angelo, Founder of Next Financial Group, Inc., Liberty Tax Service Board Member, and Author of**
 Vision: Your Pathway to Victory

Introduction

I have this crazy, almost compulsive desire to improve everyone I meet. I've found that the only way to do that is to be annoying, because if you don't get people out of their comfort zone, they don't change. If you do what you always did, you get what you always got.

Let me let you in on another secret – I'm a huge klutz. Okay, maybe it's no secret at all since I've been known to fall at the most inopportune times. I'm talking about on the ground, dust-yourself-off kind of fall. I have no problem admitting to my weaknesses because I know this - God doesn't allow anyone to skate through life. I've never met another human being, or heard of another human being, who had a completely easy life and didn't face challenges. One hundred percent of the people I've met have faced adversity most, if not all, of the time. You can get knocked down and stay down, you can complain and whine, or you can rise above it. You can choose to compete or you can just quit. It's how you deal with the adversity that's important. This is a story of falling and rising again to a new level of success.

Why should you listen to me? Because I've already developed more than 800 millionaires, and I'm the CEO of the fastest growing tax franchise system in the universe, Liberty Tax Service. My career started at H&R Block where I worked hard as a hired hand to become a regional director. From 1969-1981, the company grew from 3000 to 9000 offices. I then founded Jackson Hewitt and grew that company from 6 to 1400 offices between the years of 1982-1997. After splitting with the company that bears my name, I went on to found Liberty Tax Service in 1998, which now operates almost 5000 offices in the U.S. and Canada. This kind of growth doesn't just happen by chance.

Whether or not taxes are your thing or you dream of something else, by following my principles you will learn to set the standards in your own business; to challenge yourself and others to break boundaries. You'll learn to improve each day though communication, monitoring results, and create raving fans. Finally, why are you interested in succeeding in business at all if you're not having fun? Liberty's story can become your own story of giving and receiving loyalty, contributing to a winning team, and enjoying the journey again.

Why am I writing this book? Mainly, for my 11th principle: The Fortunate Must Give Back. I want what's best for every human being I meet. Whether or not that means joining me at Liberty, this part of my journey is about improving you - my crazy desire to annoy and challenge you - in any business you choose, with the hope that you will achieve all that you are able to achieve and then give back to others.

Part One: Set the Standard

John Hewitt

"He ambled through the course... and won!"

Chapter 1
Challenge Ourselves, Challenge Each Other, Break Boundaries

As a kid, traditional school bored me. In my opinion, it bores anyone with half a brain. My teachers disliked me because I was so argumentative. I didn't trust them. I didn't always believe that they were correct. Even if they were teaching the same thing over and over again, it's very rare that a teacher would go the whole year without making a mistake. I would mention that mistake in front of everyone. Most teachers don't like being told by a kid that they are wrong.

With my peers, I didn't fully fit in either. I was both a brainy kid (who never took a book home) and an excellent athlete, so neither group completely accepted me. Even though I was an outcast, my teachers and fellow students did respect me and I was regularly picked as the captain of the baseball, basketball, and football teams. I have always been a leader. One of the things people say about me is that I'm cocky. I once asked an old college friend, who I hadn't seen for 25 years, "What is the one thing you remember about me?" He replied, "Your self-confidence. You are the most self-confident person I've ever met."

In her book, *Let the Magic Begin*, Cathy Lee Crosby refers to the Bliss Zone™ as that "inner sanctuary of pure energy and creativity where life just 'flows' through to the very core of your heart. It's living from that place of seemingly no effort, where action is taken because one intuitively knows it's right."[1] A place we all knew as children where pure energy, creativity, and joy abound. We live in an age of bliss until we're about seven or eight years old and then everyone just beats us down. Our parents, our enemies, our friends, our teachers. They tell us that we can't be President of the United States or we can't go to the moon. They tell us we can't be a superhero. One of the differences between normal people and me is that they never beat me down. They never got to me. I always thought I could be successful and rich.

Would you believe me if I told you that you can be successful and rich? You can find your bliss zone again.

Setting the Standard – My Foundation

It was Christmas day, I was four years old, and mom knew she had an entrepreneur on her hands. I hadn't even started kindergarten, but I knew the value of a dime. My parents bought me a sled and before noon on Christmas, I went next door and sold that sled for ten cents. It was my first entrepreneurial venture. Two years later, as a six year old, I was fanatical about the game of chess. Dad and I used to play and he commented on my passion for winning the game. That competitive fire was fueled at an early age and unlike many others, I never stopped believing that I could win at any game I chose.

My father, Dan Hewitt, was a frustrated entrepreneur. He had a desire to run his own business, but had bills that needed to be paid now. My parents married young and had children right away. I was the first, born in 1949 between Dad's sophomore and junior years of college. Four siblings followed soon after.

While dad didn't have enough money to start a business, his main priority was financial independence. He worked full-time in finance in Hamburg, New York, ran a small income tax business on the side, and completed graduate school. Dad was successful by any standard, and for as long as I can remember, he wanted to work for himself and be his own boss. Dad hoped to buy an H&R Block (hereafter known as Block) franchise and I enrolled in a tax school to work with him and make some extra money. I discovered that I had a knack for this. When you find something you like and you are good at, then it doesn't seem like work at all.

Unlike regular school, I loved doing taxes because I could argue. People think taxes are just black and white, but they aren't. There is room for judgment and finding ways to help people. By asking questions and digging for deductions, you can save people money and make a difference in their lives. This was also a time when tax preparers didn't have computers or even use calculators. I was very good at math and fast at multiplication, so this work came naturally to me.

From Chess to Checkers – Mastering the Fundamentals

Management consultant and author, Peter Drucker, is famous for teaching about the importance of execution in business success; focusing on a few activities to produce significant business results. My father also reiterated the importance of mastering the fundamentals for maximum execution. Just like

a baseball team practices hitting, running, and pitching, those early years I practiced the fundamentals of the tax business in order to be the best at execution, probing and digging for deductions to get clients the maximum return.

My family was very poor at the time and my best friend, Gordon D'Angelo, was even poorer. After two years of doing taxes, I recruited him to work with me at Block. I told Gordon that we needed some people called "checkers," which was basically using an adding machine to check the accuracy of a return. For both of us, it was a great way to earn some extra cash.

At the time, neither one of us realized that this business would set the foundation for the rest of our lives. Gordon went on to become one of the best salesmen I've ever met, an initial investor at Jackson Hewitt, and founder of NEXT Financial. Today, he sits on the Board of Directors for Liberty Tax and while he never learned to love taxes the way I did, he became an extremely successful entrepreneur and visionary. We are still close friends today and I consider Gordon to be one of my most loyal confidants and advisors.

Hired Hands - When You Work for Someone Else, You Work for Yourself

Like my father, you may be born with an entrepreneurial spirit, but have bills that need to be paid yesterday. Both of us also learned the secret of being a hired hand to generate that immediate income. However we both took a different approach to being an employee in someone else's business. When you work for someone else, you work for yourself. Act as if you are the owner. Many people are just looking for a nine-to-five job. These are not the partners I am looking for at Liberty Tax today. You will learn how to succeed when you are willing to first work for others and act as if you own the business.

I must confess that up until the age of 24, I was immature. I didn't really grow up until then, when my girlfriend (who I had been dating for eight years) and I broke up. I was heartbroken. Until that point, I was a brat. I was a self-proclaimed bum and I just hadn't matured yet. I worked for Block during the tax season and I taught tax school during the fall. I also played poker at the University of Buffalo to make money. I had a great life being a bum, or so I thought at the time. I collected unemployment from April 16 until I started teaching tax school in the fall. After the break up, however, I became more committed to finding a full-time job. I decided that my life wasn't going anywhere and God didn't put us on earth to be ordinary.

The next tax season, with hopes of higher commissions, I went to work at a more established office in Buffalo, New York, with a new perspective on being a hired hand. Late in January 1971, the district manager of that store fell behind on processing returns, had several panic attacks, and ended up hospitalized. His regional director asked me to take over and run 10 locations full-time. This meant leaving college and my parents supported me in making this decision. Even then, Dad somehow sensed that I had found my calling. I believe that his own entrepreneurial spirit kicked in, encouraging me to explore non-traditional paths to success.

Winners Do What Losers are Unwilling to Do

Now at Liberty Tax, I teach my franchise owners and employees what it takes to be winners – to be number one. I do my best to inspire my team every day, many times arguing and challenging them to do what others won't. Winners do what losers are unwilling to do, and that begins with practice and mastering the fundamentals. I compete every day.

For two seasons at Block, I held down the assistant district manager role overseeing hiring, operations, supervising the staff and becoming an expert at the basics. As a hired hand, I learned how to run a business with a mindset of an owner. Then, for the next three years, I returned to preparing taxes. I worked about 600 hours per season, writing 1000 returns and teaching tax courses during the fall. As an employee, I learned the fundamentals of the tax business while working with customers every day. This business - any business - is all about the customers. Executives make mistakes when they try to get too fancy focusing on brand extensions, cross marketing and other high-minded strategies. In your business, don't ever forget that it's all about the customers.

In my first five years at Block, I thought about starting my own tax practice several times. I saw potential in the market but this hired hand just wasn't ready. I talked with some employees and my office supervisor about challenging Block in Buffalo. I saw vast opportunity in this business; clearly the industry was going to grow. However, we never took the steps to open on our own.

Stick by Your Principles, Even When it's Inconvenient

While basic tax school was easy to complete, the school of hard knocks was about to kick in on a higher level. I left Block once during those five years. A

CPA in Lockport, New York hired me to start a tax preparation business in conjunction with his practice, hoping to attract customers at lower income levels. On my first day as part of the start-up process, I reviewed the returns from the previous year. At the end of the day I was very excited; I discovered six or seven returns with errors. We could save the customers, on average, about $1,000 each; it was a fantastic feeling. I couldn't wait to tell the CPA.

"I've found some returns with mistakes. I'll do the amendments. These customers are going to be happy to get extra money back. I bet they'll refer all their friends." The CPA replied, "Naw, I do most of these returns as a favor to these people, so we don't really want to make them think we made a mistake."

This sounded like regular school all over again. This teacher didn't like to be called out, but this time it was costing people money. I quit right then and went back to Block. Obviously, he cared more about his reputation than about doing what was best for his customers. I couldn't work for someone with that attitude. I knew that his customers would have appreciated his honesty, careful review of their returns and, of course, thousands of dollars of tax refunds.

Not only did my dad teach me to work hard, he told me that principles only mean something if you have the courage and tenacity to stick by them when things are inconvenient. That day it meant walking away from my job, after just one day, with the dishonest CPA. Today, I tell franchise owners to admit mistakes right up front and take the steps to correct them. Mistakes are a wise man's education. Customers appreciate honesty and this principle will help you grow your business through referrals and good will.

A "Take-Charge" Attitude Wins the Game

It was the summer of 1975, and I had long, curly hair to go along with my cocky attitude. While I looked like a hippie, I never smoked marijuana or did any drugs. In the late 1960s, we had experienced the last big series of racial riots in this country. The massacre at Kent State was still fresh in our collective memory, just five years earlier in 1970 (when the Ohio National Guard opened fire on unarmed college students, killing four and wounding nine others). To put this era in perspective, a friend of mine was suspended from high school for having the first Beatles haircut in our town. This was a different time, and you couldn't even wear long hair or unusual clothes for fear of reprisal.

Lots of my friends also looked like hippies and my long hair didn't play too well with Block's regional director, a very conservative man who was known to be a strict and authoritative manager. He didn't respect me and he hated my hair. Like the CPA, he cared more about policies and procedures than doing what was right for customers. Several district manager positions were available, but I felt that this man wouldn't hire me regardless of my abilities. I never bothered to apply and went back to doing returns and teaching tax courses.

Fortunately, Block changed their management and re-districted western New York that summer. The regional director, who detested me, was gone. I met the new regional director, Bill Birchmeier, and Harry Buckley, the divisional director, when they observed me teaching a tax course. Right after that, they asked me to interview for a district manager's position.

Bill interviewed me on a Friday. During the conversation, Bill said, "You know, I have this guy in Elmira I'm really thinking of getting rid of." He mentioned my hair and I agreed to cut it before tax season began, if he hired me. In the middle of the interview he stopped and said, "The heck with it—can you meet me there on Monday?" That Monday, September 25, 1975, I was the new manager for Elmira.

LINDA'S TAKE ON JOHN

"In walks our new district manager who has come from Buffalo. And he has this long hair–fuzzy hair–corduroy pants that were too short, he's skinny as a rail and he's young. Most of us are, we think, older and more sophisticated, and here is this hippie-looking thing, and he's going to be our boss! No one was ready to accept him until he started teaching, talking to us, and working with us. He took over. John was a take-charge kind of person. He doesn't really worry about whether he's accepted or not, and he didn't back then either. We quickly realized he was brilliant. We knew we could learn something from him."
- **Linda Hewitt**, *Jackson Hewitt Executive, Initial Investor, John's ex-wife*

The Parable of the Talents

There is a well-known story called, "The Parable of the Talents." It's my favorite story in the Bible about investing "talents" – also known as pieces of silver. It's masterful in that a "talent" means money, however to me, it means literal talent. Here's the story:

> For *it is* just like a man *about* to go on a journey, who called his own slaves and entrusted his possessions to them. To one he gave five talents, to another, two, and to another, one, each according to his own ability; and he went on his journey. Immediately the one who had received the five talents went and traded with them, and gained five more talents. In the same manner the one who *had received* the two *talents* gained two more. But he who received the one *talent* went away, and dug *a hole* in the ground and hid his master's money.
>
> Now after a long time the master of those slaves came and settled accounts with them. The one who had received the five talents came up and brought five more talents, saying, 'Master, you entrusted five talents to me. See, I have gained five more talents.' His master said to him, 'Well done, good and faithful slave. You were faithful with a few things, I will put you in charge of many things; enter into the joy of your master.'
>
> Also the one who *had received* the two talents came up and said, 'Master, you entrusted two talents to me. See, I have gained two more talents.' His master said to him, 'Well done, good and faithful slave. You were faithful with a few things, I will put you in charge of many things; enter into the joy of your master.'
>
> And the one also who had received the one talent came up and said, 'Master, I knew you to be a hard man, reaping where you did not sow and gathering where you scattered no *seed*. And I was afraid, and went away and hid your talent in the ground. See, you have what is yours.'
>
> But his master answered and said to him, 'You wicked, lazy slave, you knew that I reap where I did not sow and gather where I scattered no *seed*. Then you ought to have put my money in the bank, and on my arrival I would have received my *money* back with interest. Therefore take away the talent from him, and give it to the one who has the ten talents.'

For to everyone who has, *more* shall be given, and he will have an abundance; but from the one who does not have, even what he does have shall be taken away. (Matthew 25:14-30 NASB)

The first two slaves received promotions and gratitude, and the master addressed them in the same way. For the third guy, it was different. It's almost as if the master expected him to be a loser, after all, he only gave him one talent in the first place. For me, the goal was to take everything I had been given and win. Win big. The lesson in this parable is that God has put you on this earth for a purpose. To go beyond what's normal and be everything you were meant to be. You were given your talents – your blessings – for a reason, not just to sit around and let them waste away.

As a district manager, I knew that to multiply our "talents," we had to innovate and grow in our service to customers. My biggest challenge did not come from running the stores or supporting franchisees. Instead, it came from fighting with the bureaucracy and inflexibility of Block corporate.

Principles Trump Policies

The Elmira region spread north to Ithaca, west to Wellsville, and south into Pennsylvania. I ran six company stores and supported five franchise locations, doing a total of 17,000–18,000 tax returns. As the manager, I heard it all. Block's answer to customer challenges was to come out with a new policy each year, sometimes to the detriment of both employees and customers. Often the policies simply didn't make sense. One dictated that managers budget just one hour per return. If a store budget called for 300 returns that week, only 300 preparer hours could be scheduled. That's patently impossible; the policy never took into account the time the office had to be staffed even if there weren't customers, nor that some of the preparer's time is spent in other activities like answering phones and researching tax questions. I ignored the policy and sent my realistic schedule to my regional director. He sent it back admonishing me to follow the policy. I wrote on the schedule that it was impossible to staff an office that way and then sent it back to him. I stood up for my principles and even though I could have been fired, I wasn't let go.

The next year, Block revised the policy to 1.4 or 1.5 preparer hours per return—a more realistic goal for scheduling. Like this example, many policies were implemented before they were thought out. The company neglected to get input from the offices. I believed that all companies should listen to their

employees and franchisees; the people closest to the customer. These principles of communication, loyalty, and contributing to the team would eventually become the foundation of my entrepreneurial successes. In my early years at Block, I learned to fight for my beliefs and that principles trumped policies.

If You Do What You've Always Done, You'll Get What You Always Got

I offered many suggestions that were turned down, but eventually implemented in subsequent years: a friend referral program; a more proactive way to contact existing customers; calling them earlier; dealing with problems right away; and simply reminding some of our customers to come back. Despite these frustrations, I helped the Elmira region grow. I won several national public relations awards, increased profit percentages, and enjoyed a good working relationship with my employees and my boss, despite the fact that I didn't always agree with him or the company.

I had a great deal of respect for Bill and his wife, Esther Guylas, a fellow district manager - smart people that had drive and ability. I made friends in Elmira who later played a huge part in my forthcoming successes: Mary Ann and Lee Lepkowski, Mary Jo and David Webster, and Linda Fervan, my future wife and partner.

Most of all, I focused on customer service and taught my managers to do the same. My customer service skills have always been superior, from the moment I was in business. Mary Ann Lepkowski was my favorite manager. With customer service, she knew I would always go over her head in dealing with an unhappy customer. Once, she had two sisters come in.

One sister had a little interest income and needed another form on her tax return that would have cost her an additional $1.50. They both worked in the same place, had the same W-2, but only one sister had a small amount of savings. One return was $15, while the other was $16.50. Back then, the average fee for tax returns was just $18; it was a different world, candy bars were a nickel.

The sister paying the higher price called and complained, saying the prices should be the same. I explained the difference – more complexity, more fees – but she still wanted the $15 return. Instead, I gave it to her for free. Mary Ann complained to me, saying the other sister would think all you had to do was complain to get your return for free. Not only didn't they complain, they

came in the next year, paid different prices, and came many years after that. My commitment to customer service has always been extraordinary, going over and above what's normal to make the client happy.

There are a number of times that customers would call me. Even if the customer was wrong, the first thing I would say is I'm sorry for the misunderstanding. I would always apologize first and make things right for the customer. Mary Ann told me that seeing me do this and watching the results, changed her management style. She started apologizing to the customer first, because she knew I was going to anyway. She improved her customer service skills, which saved me the time of overriding her.

What happens in the tax business, and it may happen in all industries working with customer service, is that the tax preparers think they're right. The customer comes in and complains, and a lot of times the tax preparer says, "I didn't do anything wrong." If the customer is upset, something is wrong. You have to do something to try to satisfy the customer, unless they are one of those rare customers that need to be fired.

MARY JO'S TAKE ON JOHN

"I had a client at H&R Block who complained about the price of his tax return. I guess from previous experience or training, I was pretty snotty with him, and just said, 'Well, that's the price. It is what it is.' John spoke to me about that; he told me I shouldn't have handled it that way. He felt our customers deserved to be treated better." - **Mary Jo Webster,** *Former Jackson Hewitt franchisee and Initial Investor*

Treat Each Job Like You're The Owner

Given my competitive nature, I wanted to advance my career. The next management level within Block was regional director. In 1978, the company began a two-to-three-year development program for promising district managers offering them training and aptitude testing before they were promoted. I had hoped to apply for the program, but Linda and I, married just one year, didn't

feel it was prudent for me to attend the training and then be relocated. Linda's three young daughters from a previous marriage had been through many changes—it wasn't a good time to move and they needed to live in the same city and state as both their mother and father.

This was a setback for me; I dreamed of being a regional director. Without attending the program, it looked as if I would be passed over for years to come. I never have regrets, however, and I didn't feel sad about it. I knew I had to make a choice and my priorities had become God, family, then business. Although when you know me it's hard to understand that it's not business, business, business. This was a family decision. I play to win, knowing that I'm not always going to win.

Two years later the Divisional Director, Harry Buckley, asked me if I wanted to interview for a position as regional director in Philadelphia. I don't know why I was chosen over people who attended the training program. Perhaps Harry considered me because he had seen me speak at a regional meeting. Perhaps Harry just realized that I had the skills and potential for the job. I believe he did see me as a maverick but, more importantly, a winner. Since then, I try to do the same each time I hire someone. I hire a person based on their strengths and attitude.

Linda and I agreed that the time and circumstances were right for a move, and the location was still close to the kids. In July of 1980, I accepted the position and became the youngest regional director in Block at the time. The region I took over had high management turnover; fourteen regional directors in thirteen years. I supervised seven new district managers and seven others who were disillusioned. The region was a mess. I enthusiastically accepted the challenge, enjoyed it, and had a great season.

In one instance, a district manager arranged to distribute $20 coupons to a Chrysler factory in Delaware. The factory agreed to place Block coupons directly into their employees' paychecks. What a great idea. It was a cheap way to advertise to 10,000 potential customers and, if nothing else, get referrals! I told the district manager to order the coupons - of course we would take advantage of this opportunity.

The Chief Operating Officer (and my manager's boss), later called and yelled at me because some franchisees just outside of my region received the coupons. They complained because the coupon went to some of their prior clients. Those franchisees gained customers too, but they focused only on the

$20 they lost honoring the coupon for previous customers. This COO told me to never give out the coupons again; he didn't care how many new customers it brought in. Like so many short-sighted, tunnel-visioned executives, he didn't understand the benefits we were getting. The numerous new customers, who redeemed the coupons, far outweighed the $20 discounts that we had to forgo.

I wasn't trying to be insubordinate. I assumed a responsibility to profitably operate the region, so I treated it like it was my own money. Remember, when you are in business for someone else, you are in business for yourself. I reaped the benefits from approaching my work as an owner: advancement, opportunity, and experience. Employees who work like owners threaten many managers, but smart managers value them, listen to them and, by all means, allow them to grow the business.

Back to the Basics – Mastering Fundamentals

The problem with the entire region was that the managers had not been executing or monitoring the basics of the business; from getting the right number of people in tax schools to watching deposits. I made a few personnel changes and refocused them on attention to the basics. I persisted in requiring the managers to monitor results, planning, and schedules. In a baseball game, the team that best executes the fundamentals of the game – hits, runs, catches, throws – wins. Business is no different. Master the basics well and success will follow.

Focusing on fundamentals turned everything around. With increases in profits and the number of returns prepared, our region placed in the top four regions in the country. During that great year, I earned the promotion I wanted. I became a Block regional director – managing 250 locations. I was very successful and very happy. Up until the age of 30, that's what I wanted to be. Performance numbers were excellent and improving, and I was proud of my employees for making that happen. Moreover, I was better off financially than I had ever been.

You'll see later that my dad had other plans for me. My success made it twice as hard for dad to convince Linda and me to leave Block. The school of hard knocks was about to reach a higher, more intense level.

JOHN'S PRINCIPLES TO LIVE BY

- Challenge ourselves, challenge each other, and break boundaries.
- Set the standard.
- Master the fundamentals.
- Hired hands-when you work for someone else, you work for yourself.
- Winners do things that losers are unwilling to do.
- Stick by your principles, even when it's inconvenient.
- A "take-charge" attitude wins the game.
- Remember the Parable of the Talents.
- Principles trump policies.
- If you do what you've always done, you'll get what you always got.

Your Challenge

What can you do today in your own business to challenge yourself, challenge your employees, and break boundaries to win your game?

I received an award from Henry Bloch in June of 1980.

Chapter 2
Be Honest, Show Respect, Have Integrity

When I was eight or nine years old in Cub Scouts, we played the "telephone" game (also known as the rumor game). That was very impactful to me. This is the game where everyone sits or stands in a straight line, the first person whispers a story to the person next to them, and it goes around the room. That day, there were 12 kids in our group and the results were just beyond belief. By the time the story got to the 12th kid, and he repeated his version, it was so incredibly different from the start, I was wondering if they were playing a joke on me.

Now, when anyone says anything to me, I wonder why it's wrong. My first reaction is it's incorrect. I have to disbelieve it to believe it. I have to have some other information to confirm that it's right before I can agree with it. I've been this way since Cub Scouts where my badge should have read, "skeptic."

It turns out being a skeptic has helped me because it's part of living outside of the box. A colleague who's known me for 20 years, Chuck Lovelace, once said, "I had an epiphany! You're always trying to take us outside the box. We get outside the box for a minute or an hour or a day, then most of us plop right back in the box. I realized that you're just never in the box." I had never thought about it that way, but it's true. There is no box that can contain me. I'm always trying to think of a way out, a way around, or a different way to hit my goal when others stop.

Part of this is differentiating facts from claims. The truth and the claimed truth are rarely the same. Where most people will just accept a statement, I phrase facts one way and claims another way. For example, many people simply believe what they read in the newspaper, or see on TV, or what they learn from their teachers in school. They assume it's accurate. I never make that assumption because I'm always thinking outside of the box. Why is this information incorrect? Virtually every time I listen to hearsay, it's inaccurate.

The truth is most human beings are just poor communicators, mainly because they are poor listeners. The only way to get an understanding of what another person said, that the two of you can agree upon, is if you re-state it in your own words. Even then it can sound different. It's the telephone game all over again. More specifically, things that are too hard to believe are usually

not accurate, so you have to take everything with a grain of salt. In business, I've found that most people exaggerate, especially about their own abilities or biases.

For example, a Block manager once made the blanket statement that all people in Pittsfield, Massachusetts hate picnics. We were discussing fun ways to give back to customers and employees. Block's system was to hold picnics for families with games, water balloon tosses, three-legged races – the whole works. According to this manager from Pittsfield, for some reason his entire city despised picnics. I remember thinking, that's bewildering. Why, in the whole country, would they hate picnics in one city? After his speech, Gordon and I sat down at lunch with him and the first thing out of his mouth – a valuable insight into people – "I hate picnics!" So, it wasn't the people in Pittsfield after all. Today, when I see that some franchisees aren't doing well in a certain part of their business, I remember this manager. That guy doesn't care, he just doesn't get it. This is a person who doesn't like picnics and his bias creates his poor performance.

If you just take statements at face value, you are going to be wrong too often. If you believe everything you hear, you will be just average and ordinary. You will be left behind. Don't be that guy who hates picnics and gets in the way of his own success.

When You Try to Minimize Your Weaknesses, You End Up with Mediocrity

In tax preparation, people are the problem, and poor communication can be costly. The errors that are made are mostly errors of omission, where people leave out information. It was always frustrating to me, being in the tax business, to watch preparers fail to dig for deductions – choosing not to go the extra mile. For example, they would ask, "Do you have any charitable contributions?" The problem is that the taxpayer doesn't know everything that is deductible.

If you are an officer in a charitable organization, for example, you may not know that you can deduct the miles, back and forth to the charity, as a charitable contribution. Mileage is one of the things most commonly missed. If you have a lot of medical expenses and are claiming medical deductions, you can claim your mileage back and forth to pick up medicine, to visit your doctor, your dentist – you can do all that.

As a regional director, I found that many preparers were very lax, almost uncaring sometimes, when digging for deductions and they were not trying to get everything for a taxpayer. My dad and I had been talking about this problem for years. Some preparers were just better than others. Customer service and quality of returns varied from office to office, preparer-to-preparer. I told my dad that the way to improve the tax process - and achieve better results - was to improve the interview between the tax preparer and the client.

In 1979, Dad invested in one of the first Apple computers by mail. (Stores didn't sell them back then.) After working on his computer for a while, he believed he had discovered the solution to incompetent or lazy preparers. Personal computers could simplify and strengthen the interview process by using a decision-tree system. "When I saw the first personal computers, I knew they could do mathematical calculations, obviously," Dad said. "But one of the first questions I asked was could they do questions and answers, like a decision tree—where you start with one question and if the answer was 'yes', you go one direction, but if the answer was 'no', you go a different direction?" This idea took a preparer who was less experienced, or less caring, and it made them into a great preparer because they had to go through all of the computerized questions. There was no way to avoid them. It made the tax return a lot more accurate and customer friendly.

For example, if you're a teacher, you are entitled to a deduction for items you buy for the classroom. That should trigger the classroom supply question to teachers from the tax preparer, but in 70-80% of the cases, it didn't. In our decision tree interview, when the client said "teacher," the computer would display the "teacher" questions.

When it got to charitable contributions, the preparer would ask, "How much did you give? Did you donate any property or clothing?" For charity leaders, we would get the mileage if they were director of the finance committee, or just a member of the committee. The decision tree would prompt preparers to deduct the mileage, back and forth, at a special rate. We would dig for deductions, prompted by a better interview, which was all directed by our computer program. The customers would come in and say, "Wow! No one ever asked me that before." As a result, customer satisfaction went up.

Together, Dad and I sat down to write this computer program, essentially creating the first tax software for a pencil and paper industry. To my knowledge, no one has ever built anything like that since. At that time, few

companies or people realized the potential of personal computers, or how prevalent they would be in the coming years. Dad sensed the great potential to use computers in the tax business and inquired about Block, which at the time, was not computerized.

Take Big Risks

During this time, my parents lived in Cherry Hill, New Jersey and Dad worked as the Chief Financial Officer for Basco Catalog Showrooms, a public company that embraced the use of computers in their operations. Basco, and many other companies at the time, used large mainframe systems in their catalog showrooms (for my young readers, who have no idea what this is, these were retail stores where you would order something on a computer terminal, and it would be sent down a conveyer belt from the back room).

In 1981, my dad took a big risk. He had saved enough money to quit his job and purchase two existing Block franchises in the Sayre, Pennsylvania area. This was a huge step for him. He was the CFO of a public company and he just quit his job saying, "I'm going to computerize taxes." Dad was finally an empty nester and as long as I can remember, he wanted to be an entrepreneur but never had the money to try it until now. Dad had saved enough to be comfortable for the rest of his life, but he decided to take a chance. This was the year I watched my dad live out his dream.

While Dad had run an accounting business before, he had never done taxes. He studied to take the Enrolled Agent exam, passed it on the first try, and began writing software on his Apple computer.

My parents planned to sell their house and, as it so happened, their home was only ten miles from my new headquarters with Block. We decided to buy their house in June and we all lived together for a few months because they weren't ready to move. This was fortuitous. During those months, my dad and I had many conversations about writing the tax program (which would become HEWTAX), yet he still couldn't convince me to take the entrepreneurial leap. I wasn't ready to take what felt like a step back when I had just been promoted, but the future was hard to ignore as Dad tested all of his programs using real tax returns.

Dad's former boss, the CEO of Basco, believed in my father and took note of his goals. As he got to know me, I also gained his confidence and he began courting me to leave Block (great seats at the Flyers and 76ers games

didn't hurt). My father was able to form a partnership with Basco to help him finance, develop, and promote the software in front of the showroom – another big coup. Getting this deal was also Dad's trump card with me, overcoming any objections I had. We now had funding, salaries, and some use of a larger company's computer expertise. I had a choice to make.

Break Boundaries

Let's pause here. If you've picked up this book, many of you are probably at a similar point in your life or long into your entrepreneurial journey. This is your fork in the road - to keep doing what you've always done and getting the same results, or to embrace your dreams and the freedom to run your own business. Forget the normal lessons you learned in school. You have to set goals that are unrealistic. God didn't put us on earth to be ordinary and you can't be all that you can be without being unrealistic. If you limit yourself by the parameters that others place on you, you will never accomplish anything worthwhile. For Dad and me, this competition was just the beginning.

In June of 1981, I took the plunge and left Block after the tax season. While the company executives had talked about introducing computers to the business, I never saw Block take any steps to make that happen. While it was frightening, I knew it was time to leave.

Demand Respect

By December of 1981, Dad and I believed our work had paid off. We were ready to roll out our interview-based program that tax season. In January of 1982, the president of Basco called and told us to stop everything. Basco was being sold to Best Products, a much larger catalog showroom. We ended up spending that tax season doing free returns for Basco employees and testing and improving the program.

During the months of purchase negotiations, no one from Best Products came to talk with us about the program. However, right before the deal closed - at the eleventh hour - a representative came to my dad, asking us to sign an agreement. Then we were supposed to take our software and go away. The agreement stated that we hadn't suffered any damages in the transition. Dad and I refused to sign. We had incurred damages: our project lost funding; we lost our salaries, and weren't permitted to showcase the software or do tax

returns, for profit, in Basco showrooms. In addition, the buyout jeopardized the negotiation of several other deals with financial groups.

Everyone Gets Knocked Down, Winners Get Back Up

When Dad and I refused to sign the agreement, Best Product's response was to hold our source code (the computer language) hostage, even though Best had no intention of marketing it or using it in their stores. We had developed the code on their Hewlett-Packard mainframe and we couldn't afford to purchase a system like theirs. To put this in perspective for today's Smartphone generation, back in the 1980s, an HP mini computer was $250,000, while an Apple was only $1800. My dad consulted with an attorney who said he didn't have a case. So he went and saw another attorney who believed in us. We sued and eventually reached a settlement with Best later that year and regained our software; however Dad and I had to rewrite the code from scratch using Apple computers at home.

Rewriting the program on a different system was one problem, but Dad and I had bigger challenges. Namely, money. We needed to find funds for our venture, find a source of income, and find a place to use the program. We were disappointed that things didn't work out, but we still knew we had something phenomenal. We refused to let the project drop. Everyone gets knocked down; winners get up again.

Early in 1982, we had solicited Block to purchase or license the software. The company had been asking for additional information, but didn't yet seem ready to commit to a new program. In March, I traveled to Kansas City, Block headquarters, to demonstrate the software, but they still hedged. They turned down the opportunity to test our software in a few of their offices.

A New Take on David and Goliath

Most of us are familiar with the story of David and Goliath. It's the account of a young shepherd, named David, who defeated a giant warrior with just a sling and a stone. The army in place, including David's own brothers, had failed at beating this behemoth and fear pervaded the camp. Most people perceive this as the story of the underdog. I see it as a story of creative weaponry. If David had gone out on the battlefield with the same sword, the same armor, the same shield as Goliath, there wouldn't be a story. He would be the 187th guy killed by this giant. Instead, David took his sling and five stones and overcame this seemingly impossible challenge.

The lesson: winners must find different weapons to fight their major obstacles. So when you're facing your own Goliath, whether it's a company or a competitor, you need to find other, superior weapons to win. For Dad and me, computers became our slings and stones. Faith was also part of the equation and our unshakable belief in our software. Today, it's probably hard to imagine a world without technology but, initially, many people opposed computerization. Feared computers, even. People couldn't picture a world with these types of machines and it is human nature to resist change. Businesses and industries resist change too, often with dire results for the shareholders and employees.

An Entrepreneur Must Sell All Stakeholders on the Vision

In April of 1982, a month before the trip to Block, I saw an ad in *The Wall Street Journal*. A tax preparation business with six offices was for sale in the Virginia Beach/Norfolk, Virginia region. The widow of the previous owner was selling it. We inquired through an attorney and they said, we can't tell you who it is. We just looked in the Yellow Pages for the tax service that had six offices and found it. It wasn't too hard to figure it out: Mel Jackson Tax Service, at the time doing 11,000 returns. Though I was busy negotiating with Block, fighting with Best Products, and rewriting our program, I still needed an income. This company could provide me with both an income and a place to use and develop the software. However, I needed to raise money if I really wanted to purchase it.

I was about to learn a crucial lesson of being an entrepreneur. It's your job to communicate and sell the vision. My friend, Gordon D'Angelo, is one of the best salespeople I've ever met. I realized that I didn't need to convince the public in raising money; I just needed to convince Gordon. When he bought into it, he would just go out and get the money.

I traveled back to Elmira and held a meeting. With Gordon's help, I told everyone there about our new company and software, "HEWTAX," and about the tax offices in Virginia. I had a taste of an entrepreneurial venture with my Dad and Basco but, at that meeting, I became a true entrepreneur the way I still define it at Liberty Tax Service today. An excellent entrepreneur is a person who has a fairly accurate vision of the future and can convince all the stakeholders to embrace that vision. The vision I conveyed was of computerized tax offices where 100% of the tax returns were done on a personal computer. Customers would benefit because they would receive faster service, a more accurate final product, and the preparer would come across as more

knowledgeable because they were prompted to ask better, more in-depth questions.

While Gordon went to his friends and other people who worked with us at Block to raise the funds we needed, I contacted my friends and colleagues at Block, looking for investors, including my favorite office supervisor, Mary Ann Lepkowski, and my second favorite office supervisor, Mary Jo Webster, who lived across the street. I went there to raise money without Gordon. They were the only investors, besides my dad and I, that I brought in.

I was so flattered because Mary Ann has seven children, and her husband Lee worked in the prison system in New York as a teacher. He fought a negative attitude his whole life because he dealt with prisoners every day. In the meantime, Mary Ann had so many children that she didn't have a full-time job. She just worked part-time for me at Block. They didn't have a lot of money. I went to see them and they came up with $10,000. I was so touched because they had to get a second mortgage on their house to invest that money.

The Lepkowskis had been talking to the Websters and they both told the other that they would invest $5000. Each of them secretly wanted to have the upper hand, so unbeknownst to the Lepkowskis, the Websters came up with $7500. They had only two children, so they had more flexibility. In the meantime, the Lepkowskis put in the whole $10,000. They won! The good news is that $10,000 ended up being worth $4 million. And the $7500 was worth $3 million.

We changed the lives not only of Mary Ann and Lee, but all of their 7 children, and their 19 grandchildren. They are all wealthier for generations to come just from that one investment. Their net worth was probably $30,000-50,000 in 1982, when they made that investment. To date, I've developed more than 800 millionaires. At that time we had 12 original investors, all who eventually became millionaires.

These people had the foresight to share my dream and invested, despite the risk, and regardless of the fact that some of them had been doing tax returns by hand for years: Gordon D'Angelo, Mary Jo and David Webster, Lee and Mary Ann Lepkowski, Sue Ventresca, Paul Grunburg, Fran Viellette, Walt Finch, Velma Frukin, and Steve Mosher. Dan and Mel Hewitt (my mom and dad), Ellen Hewitt, my sister, and Linda were among my first investors, putting their money and, more importantly, their time and belief toward my dream.

Without the support of these dedicated people, my own version of David and Goliath may have turned out very differently.

CASTING THE VISION

"No one had any money at all really...including John. I just felt he was going to succeed no matter what he did; he just had that kind of bearing about him. He was confident in his ability and confident with himself. He knew exactly where he was going." - **David Webster, *Jackson Hewitt Initial Investor, Board Member, and Former Franchise Owner***

"I was a little reluctant; it was like a pig in a poke. I knew what kind of risk he was taking to move to Virginia Beach and sign all these personal guarantees with the bank and what have you... I figured if he could do it, so could I."
- **Lee Lepkowski, *Jackson Hewitt Initial Investor and Former Franchise Owner***

"My husband's reaction was interesting. He sat back and listened to John and Gordon. He never said a word or asked a question the entire meeting. At the end, he turned to me and he said, 'I hope our two sons grow up to be like these guys.' He had such a warm feeling about John and Gordon. It was such a vote of confidence, so I knew I could invest."
- **Fran Veillette, *Jackson Hewitt Initial Investor, Board Member, and Former Franchise Owner***

Block turned down the HEWTAX system, opting to go with Texas Instruments who let them test their computer applications free of charge. On August 14, 1982, Linda and I moved to Virginia Beach and closed the deal for Mel Jackson Tax Service. My dad remained in New Jersey, assisted with the software rewrite, and administered HEWTAX, which we licensed to Mel Jackson.

Although it would take years to achieve it, we had just launched the first successful national competitor to Block. I was CEO of my own tax company, however small, and I figured if I couldn't get Block to join me, I could beat them. That drive of competition, to beat the big guy, to take down Goliath, motivates me to this day.

HEWTAX CORP.

P.O. BOX 2534
CHERRY HILL, N.J. 08034
(609) 933-3703

February 19, 1982

Kay Barthelmess
H & R Block
4410 Main Street
Kansas City, Missouri 64111

Dear Kay,

I have attached a list of the advantages our software offers.

As I indicated, we have been preparing tax returns in our de-
bugging process. Thus far, we have saved money on over 50% of these
returns. The average savings per taxpayer is over $200. We have also
amended 9% of the returns with an average savings of $297.

As I said, we can now do approximately 85% of all individual
federal returns. By next tax season we expect to be able to prepare
97 - 98% of all individual federal returns.

I look forward to being able to give you a demonstration soon.

Sincerely,

John T. Hewitt

cc: Tom Bloch

JTH/emh

TELE-TAX

JOHN'S PRINCIPLES TO LIVE BY

- Be honest, show respect, have integrity
- When you try to minimize your weaknesses, you end up with mediocrity
- Challenge yourself, challenge others
- Break boundaries
- Demand respect, not liking
- Everyone gets knocked down, winners get back up
- A new take on David vs. Goliath
- An entrepreneur must convince all stakeholders to embrace the vision

Your Challenge

What are the unrealistic goals you need to set to break through boundaries in your own life?

Danny getting ready for the school of winning, courtesy Julio.

Chapter 3
Attitude is a Matter of Choice

I've heard many people say that they want to give their children more than they had growing up. That never entered my mind. I grew up poor and I grew up fine. When I was in middle school, I had two pairs of jeans. I would wear one pair to school, while my mom was washing the other pair for the next day. I see too many children just handed stuff for nothing. Here's a fancy car – here's this or that - and the kids just turn into useless losers.

As a father, I'm a big believer in tough love. I challenged my son, Danny, from the very beginning and he will tell you that I made him work for everything. If he wanted to go to the amusement park with his friends, I would never just hand over money. I made him do chores, like mow the lawn, to earn his own way. I want my children, my franchisees, and all of my employees to understand the value of hard work and a winning attitude. Attitude is critical.

Be Like Julio
When Danny was 5 years old, watching his soccer games were like watching a swarm of bees. The only two players that sometimes stayed in position were the goalies. The others ran around the field, wearing their shin guards, kicking each other. Danny shied away from that (acting like a sissy, like most of the kids on the team) because he didn't want to get kicked. So I would try to bribe him to be more aggressive by paying him 25 cents every time he just touched the ball.

Danny went from sissy to maniac in middle school, and I believe I have a kid named Julio Rodriguez to thank for that. By this time, Danny switched from soccer to basketball and there was this crazy scrapper, Julio, who dominated the court. As parents, we couldn't take our eyes off of him. He wasn't the biggest kid on the team or the fastest, but he would rather die than lose. You see it in players like Michael Jordan and Dennis Rodman - a win or die-trying attitude. Julio had that. He was fanatically committed to winning on the basketball court and I used to tell Danny, "look at Julio, watch Julio, be like Julio." Danny finally got it. Winning is a choice: to focus, work harder than

anyone, and become a crazy scrapper in the game of basketball or the game of business. Just like Julio.

My favorite phrase in the whole world is, "only losers need excuses," so I try to never give excuses for any mistake I make. When I do something wrong, I own up to it and learn to make better decisions the next time. I don't bother giving excuses. Show me a good loser and I'll show you a loser because they've had so much practice. I'm incredibly driven and I'm a horrible loser. I think this is fairly common among people who are successful. When you set out on a path to achieve something, in my opinion, you either win or you lose. There is the joy of winning or the despicable, loathing feeling of losing. To me, the joy of winning is great – but it's not as emotional. On a scale of 1-10, winning is an emotional 8, but losing is a 10 because it's so much worse to lose. It's more *emotional* for me to lose. So I'm being driven twice – the joy of winning and the loathing of how I feel when I lose.

Attitude is a Matter of Choice – You Make the Right Choice

Becoming a small business owner in 1982, I had a win or die-trying attitude. Perseverance is the number one most important ingredient in success. My family's future was on the line, as well as our investors' money. This was game time on a whole different level. A small company named Mel Jackson Income Tax Service, was one of the only challengers to Block in the southeast Virginia region with multiple locations.

It was one of those small businesses that had "potential," which means it also had many challenges. The business was founded in 1960, operated six offices, and had a good customer base in the community, doing approximately 11,000 returns. The owner had passed away six years prior, leaving the company to his widow. By the time she put the stores up for sale, the business was losing revenue and customers.

The investors and I bought the firm for $395,000. We agreed to pay $75,000 down and $320,000 over the next five years. It was exciting to see the people who rallied to invest in us start this new venture. While Dad and I had a dream of computerizing taxes, it was unclear how we were going to monetize this. It seemed like we could make money with our software, but now we had a place to test our theory.

I feel a great respect for people who go out and start new businesses, like Steve Jobs with Apple, Jeff Bezos with Amazon, or Fred Smith starting Federal

Express – they create whole new industries. I just copied Block and executed better. At that time, it appeared that Block had no intention of ever computerizing taxes, so this was a chance to take everything I learned as a Block tax preparer and regional director, and create a superior system.

Computerization was one of the major things, although it was the little things that set us apart. I've just always lived in this age of bliss; I knew I was going to be successful, and now I was back on the path. When I was writing the computer code for the first and last time, I was like a fish out of water. Over a 12-year period, I had just focused on taxes. I started as a tax preparer and ended as the youngest H&R Block Regional Director, managing 250 offices. For one year, however, all I did was write a computer program. Going back to running a tax office was like re-entering my comfort zone. I was very confident running brick and mortar offices and I had no doubt I would be massively successful. What I didn't realize is that we would face immediate adversity.

Winners Face Challenges

Two key people, year-round employees, helped run Mel Jackson. When we researched the business, trying to decide whether or not to buy it, I spoke to both of them several times. They assured me that they would stay on and work for us. The day we closed the deal, however, they quit giving a week's notice. I told them, "Today is your last day. You can leave now." They set up competing tax practices and took some employees with them. They also took our customer list in a clear attempt to steal the customer base we purchased.

Right after they quit, we faced another challenge, finding new office space. We knew we had to move because the lease was up. The current location looked like a warehouse and tax returns were processed in an industrial, assembly line fashion. Linda describes it as "something out of the dark ages." Linda remembers, "There were rows of tables from one end to the other... no partitions, nothing. The preparers sat on one side of the table and the customers on the other side... all lined up together."

Bottles of whiteout were kept on hand to correct mistakes on forms because preparers used ink pens. The rest of the world used pencils and erasers. They didn't even keep copies of tax returns, which up until that point, I thought was a basic requirement and standard customer service. Even today, tax preparers are only required to keep a customer's name, address, and phone

number. Mel Jackson employees didn't even use a copy machine; they wrote this contact information in pen on carbon copies.

Mary Jo Webster and Mary Ann Lepkowski, two of our early investors in Mel Jackson, came down from Elmira to help us move boxes, haul tables, and do anything else that needed to be done. Because we couldn't afford hotel rooms, they stayed at our house in Virginia Beach.

The biggest challenge we had to overcome solidified one of my core values today: the commitment to outstanding customer service. Prior to our acquisition of the company, Mel Jackson clearly had not taken a customer service approach to the business. Customers sometimes waited all day to have their tax returns prepared. The previous owner's wife was known to take her small, white dog to work, growling and barking at customers. It's surprising that anyone came back. Somehow, through this time, I knew we could make the necessary changes and keep most of the prior customers. This business would grow, but it needed an overhaul on many levels, starting with the right attitude.

Find and Cultivate Winners

Sandy Raiter was, and still is one of those people with the right attitude. We were able to retain about 25 of the 50 original, part-time Mel Jackson employees, including Sandy, who still works for me today. In the beginning, she refused to work on a computer. She was mortified. Back then, people thought they might break a computer if they just touched it. Like many of the employees there, this was the first time Sandy had ever worked with a computer and she was a die-hard pencil and paper preparer. Sandy said, "Sometimes, when you'd switch disks, you'd lose the tax return and have to start over again. I thought, I am never going to use that computer! It's not going to stick."

One day her manager, Joy Brooks, told me, "You have to talk to Sandy; she's worried that she's going to get fired." So I took her out to breakfast and I told her she had a job for life and she never had to use a computer, if she didn't want to. What I valued most was her relationship with her customers. While Sandy didn't have the technical skills then, she did have the right attitude and overcame her skepticism. Without telling anyone, that summer she bought a computer for her home, practiced on her own, and became an avid computer user.

In the 1980s, however, Sandy wasn't the only one to balk at these new ideas. In fact, the 1980s computer system, rudimentary by today's standards, represented a far more sophisticated way to prepare tax returns than anyone working in the offices had experienced. To ease the transition, I made computer use optional for all returning employees including Sandy. New tax preparers, however, were required to use it. No excuses. Every first year preparer had to use this system because the computer prompted them to be more thorough and to ask better questions. The computer never missed any deductions.

The truth is, even if I wanted to, we couldn't afford to make computer use mandatory. I envisioned putting a computer on every desk, but the Apple II systems cost about $1,800 each, making it impractical for the near future. This became an issue in the offices. Once the employees overcame their fears and realized the benefits of using the software, they came in early racing to claim a desk with a computer.

Winners Stay Focused

From 1982-84, Linda and I were the only year-round employees. We acquired a Small Business Administration loan to help with expenses over the summer, when the tax business generates little revenue. One of the provisions of the loan required that Linda and I could not earn more than $24,000 combined. We borrowed $25,000 on credit cards at an 18% interest rate. We were making a small salary, but we didn't have many sales, and we were just finishing our fight with Best (new owner of Basco) to retain access to our software. We didn't even have any dining room or living room furniture. Those early days were tough, economically, but we focused on the future knowing that our hard work would eventually pay off. We didn't realize that the $25,000 loan would someday become worth 10 million dollars.

THE EARLY DAYS

"We didn't have a lot, just the business. We sold everything we had to make the initial investment. John is a risk taker. I am much more conservative. But I had all the faith in the world in John. We didn't have much of anything, but we had potential."
- **Linda Hewitt**

"John always had this bearing about him...he was successful. Even at the infancy of the company. We'd go down there (to Virginia Beach) and we'd go out to lunch or dinner at nice places and he would always pay the bill. If John was struggling, like we were, you never knew it. John always carried himself as if he were well off, as if he knew exactly where he was going, and as if nothing could deter him from his goal." - **David Webster,** *Former Jackson Hewitt Franchisee, Board Member, and Initial Investor*

You Cannot Please Everyone

Winners understand their value. Study after study has shown that customers are willing to pay more for great service. When a company is providing that to their customers, owners should never devalue their product. Businesses that try to appease every customer with their prices invariably lose money. Honoring all competitors' coupons is good business. Today, Liberty Tax honors all coupons by all competitors, *always*. However, undercutting competitors by undercharging for a company's services can be suicide for profits.

Perhaps it was to make-up for the growling dog on the premises, but for some reason the former owner of Mel Jackson was seriously undercharging for the company's services. The average fee for a tax return was about $30 compared to Block's $45 or $50. Over the first two years, I gradually increased fees, bringing them more in line with the industry standard. It was time to get back to business basics because to completely computerize, the company needed to secure more funding and increase profit margins.

By 1985, Mel Jackson was stable enough to acquire a bank line of credit. All 12 of the original shareholders had to sign a personal guarantee on that loan, which showed their level of faith in us. We were able to pay off the SBA loan and Linda and I were able to make a fair salary. We added offices each year and made modest profits for the first three years, growing from 6 offices in 1982 to 21 in 1985. Each year, we refined our operations and our computer system, which was unique in the tax business in the early 1980s, based on software written by my dad and me. I wanted the company to grow faster, but with limited resources I could only add a few stores per year and still maintain a high quality of service. My goal was to be bigger than H&R Block (9000 offices at the time). At this pace, we weren't going to get there in my lifetime.

It was time for yet another change.

The Advantages of Ownership

There are three certainties in life: death, taxes, and change. In business, if you are not changing and growing, you are floundering or dying. So I made the obvious choice that I should have made earlier and that was to franchise. My friend, board member and initial investor, Fran Veillette, tells the story best, "We had already paid for the company, got it all paid off. And the original plan was to expand on the east coast. We were going to use Virginia Beach as a nucleus and expand out from there to Maryland and then North Carolina. We wouldn't jump around, but just take advantage of the advertising, newspaper, and television and go from county to county. It would take us–I don't know how many years–to saturate the coast. Then John came back and said, 'You know what I think we should do is franchise. We must franchise.'"

Why franchise? A franchisee brings two major factors to the table: money and time. Management time. Would you rather deal with an owner or an employee when doing business? An owner has "skin in the game," caring deeply about customer service and maintaining a winning attitude. While an employee shows up to collect a paycheck, an owner stays late to build a future. Less than two percent of employees act like owners, but most owners act like owners. I saw ownership/franchising, as the key to our company's growth, raising capital, and providing a system to make others rich. Now I just had to convince our investors and potential owners.

Create a System that is Equal or Better

In September of 1985, I hired one of my seasonal tax preparers, Carolyn Buzek, as a full-time manager. She had been a director of a small local charity and she became our director of franchising, focusing on strategy and creating disclosure documents with our attorney, Carl Zwisler, former Chief Counsel of the International Franchise Association, one of the few attorneys at the time specializing in franchising. Carl said, "I remember John was extremely well prepared and strategic in his approach. He had an industry background, and had a clear idea of how to differentiate his program from the competition. I had no experience with the tax return preparation business and he patiently taught me about it, while listening to many different suggestions I offered about preparing the franchising program."

Don't get me wrong - I didn't impress everyone. We had an office supervisor named Faye Jones. I remember delivering supplies with her in early January after we had doubled the number of Mel Jackson offices. She said, "For awhile I didn't think that you guys were going to get it together, but it looks like you're going to make it." Again, there are two points to winning and losing that motivate me - those who bet on you and those who will cut you down; supporters and detractors. Just like I hate losing, the doubters are almost as motivating for me as the people who believe in me. Proving my skeptics wrong is an important part of my drive.

At that time, half of Block's locations were franchised. This system grew their business and I knew it would help ours as well. The question became who was going to become our first franchisee? Who would tell the story that this system works? So I said, "Let's sell our company stores. We can raise money from that. I won't have to run them anymore, and I can focus on franchising. This would also give us testimonials of people who are working in the system and know that the system works for them."

Remember, since that time I've helped more than 800 people become millionaires. Back in 1985, however, I was still learning the process myself and I offered to partner with other employees who were unsure about ownership. Most of them had the skills and had been running the offices well. The only thing they lacked was the confidence to conduct business on their own.

In March of 1986, we called a meeting for those interested in becoming franchisees and all office supervisors. We had our documents ready and

introduced the concept of buying franchises. Most of the office supervisors and a couple of the seasonal employees came and we were able to sell all of the stores to existing employees except for one in Chesapeake and three on the Peninsula region of Virginia. These partnerships took shape in different ways and many formed relationships that are still in business today.

Break Boundaries - From Employees to Owners

One group was especially creative. My COO, Walter Ward, helped facilitate deals; putting together a group of about a dozen employees who called themselves Employees, Inc. Together, they invested and bought six offices in Portsmouth, Suffolk, and Chesapeake. One of the initial investors in this group was Ethel Smith, who was always like a mother to me. Today, she is almost 90 years old and her family went on to own 20 franchises with Jackson Hewitt.

> John was my favorite boss. He was a sweetheart. I admired him and I think he's a very brilliant man. Right out of high school I went to work for the government in account maintenance. Back then we didn't have any money to go to college. We worked very hard and took it seriously. I spent 40 years with the government and worked my way up to budget analyst. Then I went into the tax business and I loved it! I don't love paying taxes, but I enjoyed preparing taxes and working with people. I invested with John because I just knew he would be a success. We certainly had our high and low times, but I wasn't afraid to invest, because I had faith in John. I wouldn't trade any of these experiences and working with John changed my family's life. You never forget the people. – **Ethel Smith, *Jackson Hewitt Employee, later Franchisee***

Another woman, Signe Tucker, of Chesapeake felt too timid to invest on her own. Like many employees, her biggest liability was a lack of confidence. So my ex-wife, Linda, and I bought half of the store and she bought the other

half. It worked perfectly. She and her husband went on to fully acquire the store three years later. They had tripled their revenue and they bought us out. This worked out well because they kept all the profits and we gained a great franchise with very little investment, less than $20,000. I was making more than that each year on this office alone.

We also approached Jenny Ward, one of our preparers, about purchasing the territory she was then managing. Jenny recalls, "Here I was, a housewife from a small community in Ohio. You want me to do what? How in the world can I ever run a business? He was actually a partner in the territory we owned over there. John made me believe I could do it."

Mistakes are a Wise Person's Education

I have no regrets in life, however, that doesn't mean I haven't made a zillion mistakes. I have. One of the biggest mistakes I made in business was not turning to franchising sooner. Once we embraced franchising, this chess move became the crucial game changer for our business.

Virginia's Peninsula region turned out even better because Jenny acquired the three stores there and became partners with Carolyn Buzek and me. We each owned one third of the business. Carolyn and I put up the money, and Jenny did the work and received a salary. We grew this to half a dozen offices and - after a couple of years - we sold those offices because Jenny's husband, Ken, had gotten a job in Raleigh- Durham, North Carolina. I sold my part and made a nice profit. Carolyn and Jenny continued on as partners and bought up all of Raleigh-Durham. They had about 10 stores in that market and then bought Greensboro, Winston-Salem, and they bought another dozen stores. They would go on to become one of our top 10 franchisees, with more than 20 stores. Eventually, they moved back to Ohio, where they had grown up, and sold their stores for millions of dollars.

The Southeastern Virginia market was sold out. One of our franchisees, Virginia Whitt, had a manager named Rob Stepp who was moving to Richmond. Everyone liked Rob, so Linda, my now ex-wife, and I partnered with four local franchisees to buy territories in that city. Our partners included Buddy and Virginia Whitt, John and Sharon McCormick, Dave and Irene Odebralski, and Richard and Betty Hackworth. Each couple put in 20 percent. Again, this worked out perfectly because several years later, the manager wanted equity in the business. I said, "Absolutely, I always want the manager

to have equity because they work harder if they have equity in the business." The others, however, voted it down. Three investors didn't want to give up any of their equity, so I sold him my 20 percent and made another nice profit from my investment. This worked out well for him – he got a higher percentage of equity in the company than if he had five partners.

Winners Listen to Other Winners

Mel Jackson went into the 1987 tax season as an operating franchisor, but was about to face another challenge and a name change. Carolyn opened an office in Durham, North Carolina, and this was the first time we did business outside of southeastern Virginia. The problem was that the brother of the original owner also operated three tax offices in North Carolina - also called Mel Jackson. This sparked a lawsuit when we applied federally for the name. "Mel" was fine – and legal – when we were small, but expanding meant outgrowing this name.

My nature is to compete and fight for what's mine. I resisted changing the name at first. I didn't want to confuse the customers who had been coming to Mel Jackson since 1960. But both Carolyn and Fran Veillette talked me out of this battle. They never loved the name. Mel Jackson reminded them too much of "Mel's Diner" from the 1980s popular television sitcom, *Alice*. They said the name was "too country" and "not professional enough" for a nationwide tax preparation franchise.

Once the lawsuit was filed in North Carolina, I agreed to find another name. I wanted to focus on franchising and growing the business. I had no interest and no time for a court fight, and neither did my managers or the Board of Directors. The company surrendered the right to use the name Mel Jackson Tax Service.

It was Fran who played around with names and, finally, put together Jackson Hewitt. Fran recalls passing it by several other friends. "Everyone thought it was wonderful. They thought it sounded sophisticated. We still kept Jackson so we'd have some recognition there. I mentioned it to John and he wasn't sure about it. My son, who by this time was a lawyer, said 'Mom, you're brilliant.' I'll never forget that feeling, my son saying I was brilliant."

Indeed she was, and all the managers thought Jackson Hewitt was a great name. It was important to me that we keep "Jackson" as part of the name because we didn't want to lose the Mel Jackson name recognition and customers.

Remember Julio?

As I look back on those first five years with Mel Jackson, I realize that we were all passionate, intense scrappers playing a game that naysayers told us we would never win. Our employees went from fearing computers to fighting over them, and our software was getting better and better. We had expanded from 6 to 22 stores and began operating outside of the southeastern Virginia area known as Hampton Roads. Plus, we started selling franchises.

In the game of business, we were like Julio, fighting for our place at the top. Win or die trying. No excuses. We never guessed that a very surprising ally would help catapult Jackson Hewitt to the second largest tax preparer in the country. Julio – meet the IRS.

JOHN'S PRINCIPLES TO LIVE BY

- Be like Julio
- Attitude is a matter of choice – you make the right choice
- Winners face challenges
- Find and cultivate winners
- Winners stay focused
- You cannot please everyone
- The advantages of ownership
- Create a system that is equal or better
- Break boundaries – from employees to owners
- Mistakes are a wise person's education
- Winners listen to other winners

Your Challenge

How can you be like Julio in your business?

Part Two: Improve Each Day

KEY INDICATORS

DOW Friday close	+ 25.74	2,904.95
DOLLAR N.Y. close	+ 1.13 yen	151.70
GOLD Comex close	− 50 cents	$361.10
BONDS 30-yr treasury	+ 4.10%	8.50%

RONALD J. COLLERAN/Buffalo News

John Hewitt in front of his office at Bailey and Kensington avenues, one of 230 nationwide.

As a tax preparer, John Hewitt is a chip off the old H&R Block

By RICK STOUFFER
News Business Reporter

John Hewitt loves tax season. He loves the crowds, the forms, the receipts, the clicking computer terminals.

But most of all, he loves the thought of some day overtaking his former employer in the tax preparation business: H&R Block.

A Hamburg native, Hewitt is president and chief executive officer of Jackson Hewitt Tax Service, a Virginia Beach, Va.-based firm that has grown in eight years from six company-owned stores to 230 offices coast to coast — including 103 in Montgomery Ward department stores.

Jackson Hewitt added more than 80 franchise offices in 1989 alone, making it the 33rd fastest-growing franchisee in the country last year, as determined by Entrepreneur magazine. The company has six offices in Erie County, plus single offices in Lockport and Niagara Falls.

During the recently completed tax season, Jackson Hewitt processed 140,000 returns and grossed $7.5 million.

Despite the rapid growth, Jackson Hewitt remains a fly on the back of the tax-preparation leader. This past tax season Block processed more than 14 million returns through about 8,000 offices, and generated from tax preparation worldwide $547 million in gross revenues and $138.6 million in pre-tax operating profit.

But Hewitt, who experienced the Block organization from the inside for more than a decade, feels he possesses the antidote to neutralize the industry giant: electronically prepared, electronically filed tax returns. About 90 percent of Jackson Hewitt's returns are electronically filed.

"Computer to computer, electronic filing is one of the two biggest events ever in the tax-preparation business, the other being Block's formation," said Hewitt, who graduated from Hamburg High School in 1967.

"We're certainly promoting electronic filing," said Frank Keith, an IRS spokesperson in Washington, D.C.

During last year's tax-filing season, 1.9 million returns were filed electronically. This past season, ending April 15, 4.2 million were filed that way. Projections are that between five and six million returns will be electronically filed nationwide next tax season.

Of the 4.2 million filed by computer this tax season, 2.9 million came via Block.

In the IRS' Buffalo District, which includes 32 counties, 93,500 returns were filed electronically this past tax season, versus 36,000 the year before.

Jackson Hewitt obviously knows its computers. For the last two years the firm has written the IRS' electronic-filing test, basically the examination that all preparers must take to participate in the electronic program.

But Block, too, is embracing electronics. "Electronic filing is going gangbusters for Block," said Paul Mackey, a New York-based analyst with Dean Witter Reynolds who follows the Kansas City, Mo.-based firm. For the tax season just completed, all Block offices featured electronic filing.

Filing returns electronically goes hand-in-hand with Hewitt's software for preparing tax returns. Most programs basically flash replications of a computer-standard IRS forms on a computer screen, with blanks filled in by what is hoped will be a competent person.

Using Jackson Hewitt's software, called a "decision tree program," preparers are forced to ask specific computer-generated questions with literally thousands of question paths as possible, depending on how a client responds.

"The computer asks the questions that an interviewer might not think appropriate," Hewitt said.

The software, developed in conjunction with Hewitt's father, Daniel, was ready for use in early 1982. But possible deals to put the software to use fell through, including a pitch to former employer Block, for whom he had worked from 1970 to 1981. No one was biting, so the Hewitts decided to buy their own, ongoing tax-preparation business.

"We put together a group of investors and bought Mel Jackson's Tax Service for $395,000," Hewitt said. The Tidewater, Va.-based firm, in business since 1960, had six offices.

Between 1982 and 1985, Hewitt slowly expanded Mel Jackson's firm, adding 16 company-owned outlets. Then, taking a cue from Block, which franchised more than half its offices, Hewitt began franchising in 1986, starting with the original company-owned stores.

Today, Jackson Hewitt — the name change came in 1988 — has 230 offices, only one company-owned, and it is for sale.

Even with his computerized software, Hewitt admits his growth in the last eight years would have been much slower had it not been for the Internal Revenue Service introduced computer-to-computer income tax filing in 1986.

Hampton Roads, near Virginia Beach, was one of 11 markets originally selected by the IRS for electronic filing in 1987. The IRS loves the system because it cuts down on labor and storage costs. One laser disk can store the equivalent of 900,000 paper returns.

Errors also are cut substantially via electronic filing, said IRS spokesperson Frank Keith.

"Paper forms carry an error rate of about 16 percent; electronic filing's error rate is about 3 percent," Keith said.

The taxpayer also gets a return much quicker using electronic filing: two to three weeks, versus the standard eight- to 12-week wait with paper returns. And, through the use of a refund anticipation loan Jackson Hewitt offers in conjunction with various financial institutions, refunds can be issued in three days. The time drops to two days during next tax season.

For its computer-generated preparation, Jackson Hewitt charges on average about $50, about the same as Block. To file a 1040-prepared return, an additional $15 to $20 is charged. Next season, the fee will go down, a "good marketing tool," Hewitt said.

For $30, the average Jackson Hewitt customer is asked about 100 questions. About 40 minutes is needed to complete the electronic form.

While his firm is still puny, office-wise, compared to Block, Hewitt has no doubts it is someday will be an equal.

"I want to be as big as Block; I want 9,000 to 10,000 offices nationwide," Hewitt said. And he wants those offices as close to Block stores as possible.

"I learned in marketing class that the best place to be is right next to your competition."

**For More Information
Call 1-800-277-FAST**

Chapter 4
Communication, Communication, Communication

At Liberty Tax Service, I conduct management retreats several times a year. Once, when there were about 30 people in the room, I asked, "How many of you think that your supervisors or peers do an excellent job at communicating with you?" Only one or two people raised their hands. Then I asked, "How many of you think you do a good job communicating with your peers?" That time, four or five people raised their hands. They were all wrong.

Improve Each Day

When it comes to communication, no one gets it right. It's an essential part of every relationship, whether it's a marriage, a partnership, a business, or an employer and employee. I don't care if you have a Ph.D. in communications; I've never met a person who consistently listens or gets their message across. Even if you're close and you try, things are taken out of context or misheard or misstated. Communication is something that no company and probably no couple have ever mastered.

Here's the problem: human beings are communication stoppers. Every person I know wants to receive communication - they want to know everything - but they don't give communication back. Information is power and people will hoard it. Whether or not it's going to the trouble to say something or simply remembering to communicate at all, our desire to get information is greater than our desire to give it. There is no solution to our constant communication dilemma, but we can work at improving every day.

I married a woman with three daughters and tough love was also part of their communication curriculum. I'll never forget how angry our oldest daughter, Patti, was when she came home two minutes late from a date with her boyfriend (and future husband, Troy Robertson). I grounded her for two days. She knew, long in advance, that she would be punished if she came home late. I go to bed at 10:00 or 11:00 and I said to Patti, "Your curfew is midnight and I don't want to have to get up and worry that you're not here, and that

you're dead somewhere. So, all you have to do is call." Communication. If she had called, she could have stayed out later. Patti learned quickly, and she's a very timely person as a result of my guidance. But first, back to business and our lesson in communicating with the IRS on a whole new level.

If You're Not Improving, Your Competitor is Gaining

In 1986, the government launched a pilot program to test the electronic filing of tax returns in Phoenix, Cincinnati, and Raleigh-Durham. Nowadays, e-filing is routine. Then, for the IRS, this was a huge step into the future and it became a pivotal point for us and how we would expand. Our company was already ahead of the curve with computerization and electronic filing and the next year, the IRS picked Norfolk/Virginia Beach as a test area, partly because of our offices.

We had caught the attention of Lenny Holt, then Chief of Operations and Marketing Branch in the Electronic Filing Project Office of the IRS. He said our firm was, "holding its own, volume-wise" against the larger filers: Block and Beneficial. Only 7,800 returns from the Hampton Roads area were filed electronically and 5,200 of those were from our company. We did twice the number of all our competitors combined. At that time Block also charged extra for electronic filing. We included it in our fee. Overall, this was better for the customer because they didn't feel like they were being charged extra for this service we provided. It took Block and many of the independent offices more than a decade to stop charging extra for electronic filing. On April 15th, Holt and his assistant came down to Virginia Beach to watch how we ran our operation.

Because each year we had refined the computer software, we had no trouble becoming leaders in this new system. We now got customers their refunds in less than three weeks, half the time it took before electronic filing. The company experienced a thirty percent increase in volume of returns over previous years. I decided then to scrap all earlier expansion plans; we would now go wherever the IRS expanded with its electronic filing program. Plus, electronic filing would make selling franchises easier and our customers loved it. After years of hard work, everything seemed to be coming together.

If We Agree All the Time, One of Us is Useless

For most people, the idea of communicating with the IRS is on par with a trip to the dentist. We decided to take a direct approach in working with them. To become one of their test transmitters, we had to take a test. The IRS sent 50 tax returns that deliberately had 3 errors in them; we were supposed to correct the errors and send them back electronically. Instead, we found hundreds of errors. We called them back and said in a very polite way, "Which of these 200 errors are the 3 that you want us to catch?"

We tend to treat the IRS softly, and show them the respect they deserve. However, Dale McClure headed up Jackson Hewitt's technology department and was a bear-like kind of guy. He called up the IRS and told them, "Your test is horrible!" Electronic filing was small at the time and there were only a few players including Block and us. While we didn't agree on many things, every company agreed that this IRS test needed a lot of work. We offered them a different plan. We said, "Instead of sending out that test, why don't you bring it down here to Virginia Beach – spend a day or two with us – and we'll fix it for free." The IRS took us up on the offer. A day or two turned into a week and we still couldn't fix all of the problems. So, the second year we said, "Why don't you pay us to write the tests?"

For three years, 1988-1990, Jackson Hewitt was the sole provider of the Preparer Acceptance Tests (PATS), which helped to establish us as a leader in electronic filing. Developing the IRS test was not a moneymaking venture; they paid us only $30,000-$35,000 per year. Lenny Holt said, "They were so efficient. The dealings we had with them were crisp. Things worked well; we liked running ideas by them because we got honest feedback. John and his group always were cooperative, willing to help. Always very prompt and studious in their responses."

Keep Communicating the Vision

Our direct and honest communication with the IRS opened doors and helped solidify our vision for the future. During the summer of 1987, the IRS extended their program into New York State, which couldn't have been better for us. Since most of my investors, former colleagues and friends were in New York, I offered them the first chance to purchase franchises — a chance for ownership that many H&R Block employees would never have. We had wide-open availability for operating territories that Block either couldn't or wouldn't pro-

vide. I also gave opportunities for my present and former colleagues to invest or become employees.

OPEN AND HONEST COMMUNICATION

"David and I, along with Mary Ann and Lee, went to Myrtle Beach for a vacation with the kids. John and Linda came down from Virginia Beach to spend a couple days with us. John told us that New York State was in the process of getting approved for electronic filing. He just mentioned it. I guess that's how we got started. John sold us a franchise while we sat there on the beach. But — you know what good friends Mary Ann and I are — John expressed concern about us becoming business partners. He had seen business partnerships break up friendships. He didn't want us to buy a franchise if we had any concerns about that." - **Mary Jo Webster,** *former Jackson Hewitt Franchisee and Initial Investor*

"I had left H&R Block, and was out on my own preparing taxes when an acquaintance of mine, who had worked with John at Block, told me about John Hewitt. She said, 'I think you should look into this opportunity. John is getting ready to expand into the New York market. You really should get in on this.' I asked her why. She told me, 'If there is anyone who can take on H&R Block, this man can do it'. That piqued my interest. I came down to Virginia Beach, met with John, and was very impressed. He answered every single one of my questions. Nothing was a secret. He pulled out reports; he pulled out tax returns — everything. He was so open and honest." - **Donna Halligan,** *Former Jackson Hewitt franchise owner and company manager, later Liberty Tax franchisee, corporate employee and area developer*

I turned down several people who wanted franchises. Either I knew they wouldn't make it as an entrepreneur, or I knew they wanted an area in which

I wasn't ready to compete. I trusted my instincts about this and it paid off. Most of the employees and franchisees were our friends, friends of friends, prior coworkers, or former employees.

In the summer of 1988, we also completed a private placement of stock that gave the company almost $1,000,000 in capital. I was very pleased with how well we were competing in our markets. The company was ripe for expansion. We needed more managers, experienced managers. I asked my former boss, Bill Birchmeier, and his wife, Esther Gulyas, —both still H&R Block employees— to join the company.

For my money, Esther was the best on-air communicator and public relations person I had ever seen in the tax industry. Since she was great on TV: enthusiastic, knowledgeable about taxes, and fearless, I was certain her skills would help the company grow. Bill would provide the operations management experience we needed. Linda and I no longer could do everything. With the added support and experience Bill and Ester provided, we could meet our goal of doubling our offices in the next year.

Listen to the Person Closest to the Customer

As an entrepreneur, you can never make assumptions. If you are not the one in direct contact with your customers on a daily basis, you have to communicate with the person who is. Successful owners must listen to their employees. Those in authority need to pay attention to the troops on the ground just the way Lenny Holt and his team at the IRS listened to us.

Our Chief Marketing Officer, Martha O'Gorman and I once flew to Kansas City to interview a person for the CFO position. Martha asked, "What is your management philosophy?" He replied, "Ours is not to reason why, but to do or die." In his world, all the orders come from above and you are not supposed to question them. Just do it, like a good soldier. That is how many companies are run. Many CEOs issue edicts and say, "this is what we're going to do," instead of listening to the people who deal with the customer because they think they know best. It's partly because they feel if they admit that they don't know best, then they look inferior or won't be perceived as a good CEO, so they just don't listen.

I'm secure enough in my leadership to listen to employees. They are the boots on the ground and they know what the customer really wants. Whether it's a higher level of service, kid-friendly offices, or refreshments, I listen. For

example, we print out a letter that we give to every customer with their tax return. Why would I think I could do that better than the person who gives it out thousands of times? They give out two million letters with tax returns. Why would a CEO think he could create a better letter than the people who are closest to the customer? They should design the letter; we should just implement it. There are hundreds of issues like this.

Listen to Your Employees

In my company, I know the big picture better than anyone, but my franchisees and employees know the tools they need to exceed customer expectations. A good CEO will trust employees to make the right decisions - empowering them instead of just issuing automatic edicts that they must follow. To succeed, employees must feel free to make suggestions and give advice to their managers without concern for retribution. Remember, humans are communication stoppers. The managers who listen the most – and listen well - to their employees will win.

While I still believe that no one really masters communication, we worked to improve every day and set the standard. I regularly teach the importance of improving every day in the way we communicate to our customers, to our employees, and to our owners. Customers come first – always. Words aren't the only communication that a client notices. An employee's attitude, tone of voice, facial expressions and gestures are all part of the message, leading to either positive or negative results. At Liberty, an important part of our system is to call each client within 24-48 hours of completing a return. We ask for feedback on our service and if they can offer any suggestions to help us improve. Most importantly, we listen.

Negotiation – Find Out What Motivates People

Back to Patti. She was a very spirited, talented young girl and the best receptionist we ever had at Jackson Hewitt. She worked nights and weekends, an incredible employee; friendly and personable. Patti went to school to get a marketing degree and was in her senior year of college at Old Dominion University in Norfolk, Virginia. I overheard someone ask her, "Are you going to work for mom and dad when you get out of school?" She said, "No way. They're tough!" We *were* tough and she wanted to get away from that. My

goal, however, was to get her to work full-time for our company. Of course, I couldn't let her know that.

Workers like Patti are hard to find. I knew this would be a tricky negotiation, but I also knew a few things about my daughter: she was tired of school, loved a challenge, and loved to travel. So I went to her and said, "Patti, how about we make this deal. You take your last semester off of college, come and work for Jackson Hewitt. We're opening all of these offices around the country and you can teach people the system. You can travel around and it will look great on your resume. But you have to promise that you'll go back and get your degree next September."

She loved the idea! It sounded fun, she would get to travel around the country and make money. No surprise – she did a great job. During the summer, she continued working in the training department and in the fall, true to her word, she went back to school and finished her degree.

Patti came back to work for us in the 1988 tax season and ended up staying for another 10 years. The daughter who said she would never work for her parents became one of our vice presidents and took over for her mom as the Director of Training. For my part, years of training in business have taught me some communication strategies and negotiation tricks for my hardest customers: our kids.

Negotiating Our Future

In 1988, now officially renamed Jackson Hewitt, we opened 49 offices at the beginning of the tax season. Together, we more than tripled the number of electronically filed returns from the previous year to 15,900. That number represented 10% of all the electronic returns filed nationally with the IRS by all firms. We were well on our way.

I had no idea that my drive to grow quickly would lead to one of my greatest mistakes and darkest times in my career. Our next step almost destroyed us.

JOHN'S PRINCIPLES TO LIVE BY

- Improve each day
- If you're not improving, your competitor is gaining
- If we agree all of the time, one of us is useless
- Listen to the person closest to the customer
- Employees need to give the company advice
- Communication, communication, communication
- Negotiate – find out what people need

Your Challenge

Communication is key to your company's success. While you will never solve the challenges of communication, how can you improve each day?

Chapter 5
Mistakes are a Wise Person's Education

Think about how you were graded in school. You were rewarded for being correct and scolded when you did something wrong. To be innovative and extraordinary in business, you have to be willing to be wrong. If you are afraid to make mistakes, you will always just be ordinary. Remember, I told you about my predisposition for falling at the most inopportune times - right before giving a speech or just walking into the office. Normally, a fall is just a physical distraction – I try not to get hurt or take anyone else down with me. Well, my next move was a fall of a different kind; it almost bankrupted the company. Everyone I know makes mistakes and takes a spill at sometime in their lives. The difference is that winners get back up and keep going.

If it Sounds too Good to be True...

In autumn of 1988, the owners of Tax Centers of America (TCA), a Long Island-based tax preparer, called me wanting to sell their customer lists. TCA had a contract with Montgomery Ward to operate 169 tax offices in stores throughout the United States. This would allow us to acquire the list and gain access to all Montgomery Ward's locations. We wanted to grow the company and this seemed perfect. Here was an immediate chance to become the second largest tax preparer in the country, several years faster than I planned. Operating in Wards would give us inexpensive, ready-made offices. Plus, the association with a national retailer would further enhance Jackson Hewitt's name recognition. We decided to go for it and purchased the customer lists from TCA.

That tax season, Jackson Hewitt opened 197 offices in 34 states, coast to coast. We'd only sold 40 of the 169 TCA locations as franchises and had to manage the rest as company stores. We had problems recruiting and training employees from afar and had higher personnel, advertising, and operating costs than we budgeted.

Don't Quit

As we started our busy tax season, red flags starting waving everywhere. I found out that TCA, which eventually filed Chapter 11 bankruptcy, had not paid wages or even bonuses to many of their previous employees. Their employees were so angry that many tried to steal the customer base. Many of them set up their own tax practices and sent mailings to prior customers. Several former employees stood in our Montgomery Ward locations and stopped customers on their way in to the offices.

We were devastated. We didn't meet any of our volume projections and bled cash.

Walter Ewell, the former Jackson Hewitt Controller and Director of Franchise Development tells the story well. "We're busy losing money like crazy," Walter remembers. "The offices aren't doing anything. We're not even taking in what we're spending in payroll. Of course, Wards is taking in the money through their cash registers, taking their percentage and then paying us, so there's a lag time there. We have some cash flow, but not enough. All the money we raised was long gone. We're running up huge bills with the advertising agency. At one point, it became very clear that if we went even another week or two, that we would be gone. When you run slam out of cash, it's just over."

It almost was.

Don't Languish Over Your Mistakes

As an entrepreneur, you will make mistakes. What you do next will determine if you survive or not. It's tempting to beat yourself up and languish over what's happening to you. The "why me" syndrome. Get over it and start your damage control strategy. In a crisis – even one of your own making – you don't have time to whine. Instead, start making some tough decisions – fast.

Just a month after we opened in the Wards' stores, I decided that we had to close the worst performing ones – 67 of them by March 1. Wards' management was furious, but my only other alternative was bankruptcy, and that wouldn't have helped either company. We needed to strategize and fight like crazy to make it to the following January without much cash. I stopped taking a salary and cut Linda's pay. Esther and Bill gave up one salary and we reduced all the regional directors' salaries by half. Any willing employee received stock options instead of a salary.

While those cutbacks helped, Jackson Hewitt desperately needed money for the coming months. I approached some of the original investors, but several had children in college and didn't want to take the risk. My dad and I loaned the company more money, and agreed to forgo the royalties we were due from the Hewtax software.

We also survived that summer by selling franchises. Walter Ewell, our controller turned director of franchise development, and I drafted an aggressive strategy that included attending every scheduled franchise show in the country. Walt did a great job working the plan, and spent much of the summer and fall on the road.

When All Else Fails – Laugh!

When I had first met with Wards' management during the tax season to tell them we were closing some of the offices, they threatened to sue Jackson Hewitt, and wanted us out. Walt, Esther, and I made a trek to Chicago to see the Wards' managers. They were hot, "mad as fire," recalls Walt. What are our chances we're going to get through this? Walt had put together a presentation book and showed the difference in the kind of support Sears gives H&R Block with more visible store signage and better locations within the store.

Then he showed pictures of some of our locations where we were behind the women's bras in the corner next to the store bathroom with no store signage. Walt put together this argument in pictures to show that part of the reason we struggled in their stores was because Wards hadn't fully committed to the program, which was the intent of the original agreement.

Walt picks up the story from here, "So, we go into this meeting and they are just railing on us, especially this one good-looking, blond, Harvard MBA type. We're sitting there, taking this for about an hour, and I said, 'You know what this makes me feel like?' He stopped and said, 'What?' I said, 'We're kind of like a little kitty cat just laying outside the farm house resting in the sun, and a great big old coon dog comes out, lifts his leg, and pees on us. We realize what's happening and jump up and try to run in the house. When we get in the house, everyone is mad 'cause we're all wet.' I remember looking at John and Esther who looked at me like, 'Have you lost your mind?' But the guy just busted out laughing."

Walt was right – I did think he had lost his mind, but I couldn't believe that guy was actually laughing. He was human, after all. I took that opening,

and got a handshake agreement that we could open in Wards next season and an agreement that they wouldn't sue us. Plus, we got them to agree to better locations (no longer behind the women's bras), more signage, and a more co-ordinated advertising effort.

Embrace Criticism

One moment of laughter aside, we took a verbal beating from Wards that was humbling beyond words. It was during this time, however, I learned the value of embracing criticism. One of my core principles today is that mistakes are a wise person's education. The difficulty is improving and knowing how to improve without feedback. If you have to just figure out for yourself what you have to do to improve, it's a lot more difficult than if you hear it from other people and they give you guidance. While they're not always right, the truth is somewhere between how you feel and how they feel.

As a boss, it's not productive if you just sit in a vacuum where everyone just sucks up to you. Many CEOs love that, but that's wrong. Remember, if two employees always agree on everything, then one of them is useless. It's beneficial for people to challenge you and tell you when you're wrong. Occasionally, they are going to be right, as in the case of Wards. Almost every time I disagree with someone, after some thought, I realize they are at least partially right. When we're arguing, I'm trying to learn from you. It's an opportunity to improve. Most people are poor at embracing this kind of feedback. We fight off any kind of criticism. For me, Wards was entering this school of hard knocks at the advanced level. No excuses.

Being in a franchise organization, we have an extra advantage to improve because people complain even when things aren't wrong. In the corporate world, people don't want to step on toes; they don't want to get anyone in trouble, so they'll sit back and take poor behavior and violated principles without raising their hand and standing up for themselves. In a franchise organization, it's valuable that franchisees don't have that same allegiance. They will complain about everything.

Ten years ago at Liberty, I got an email complaint on April 15th - a Saturday. A newspaper reporter had called a franchisee in Los Angeles saying they were on the way to his office. He called our marketing department, fearfully, asking, "What should I say? What should I do? How do I handle the news media?" There was no one in this department that Saturday, so there was no

one to take his call. He immediately lodged a long complaint about how the marketing department should have been working on April 15ᵗʰ.

The Vice President of Marketing resisted criticism and didn't want to hear anything bad about herself. The first thing she did was attack instead of letting it sink in. She said, "This guy is a losing franchisee – one of the worst in the country. He complains about everything. He doesn't do anything. He's only doing 300 returns. Why should we listen to him?" She gave as an excuse that all of the people were in the field helping and that's why they weren't in the office.

I replied, "We don't train anyone to handle the media? Why not? Sometime, some year the news media is going to come to your office during tax season and you have to know how to speak with them. Secondly, why don't we have a list of things to do – to say or not to say - to give the best interview possible and help the most people? We can modify our system – use this complaint as the tip of the iceberg – to improve our process or we can just ignore it and say the guy's a jerk." Today, we have a public relations training system for our franchisees and lengthy documentation of what to do when approached by the press, thanks to our willingness to embrace criticism and learn from our mistakes. You need to look for ways to improve. All human beings say they want to improve and can handle constructive criticism, but no one really wants to hear it. No one takes it well. So you need to learn to embrace criticism and learn something from each situation.

We Learn by Trial and Error

Most of the summer Wards vacillated about letting Jackson Hewitt enter the stores and some of our board members felt it might be better to get out of those locations. I believed that salvaging the relationship with Wards was a priority. Name recognition, national presence, ease of selling franchises, availability of locations and all the other reasons we accepted the challenge in the first place still continued as strong positives. Also, Wards would be less likely to sue us if we continued the relationship.

I worked on mending our relationship because I focused on the future. Potential franchisees were more likely to do business with us if they already had locations and wouldn't have to be concerned with year-round rent. By the end of the tax season, the remaining stores showed great results. The locations we hadn't closed generated more revenue for Wards than TCA had the

previous year with twice the offices. By 1989, we had a new Wards' contract in place and sales were doing better. Still, every day I watched our cash flow and tried to come up with ways to keep the business going in its current form.

In addition to operating costs, we owed vendors money. The largest was to an outside advertising agency, which handled all of the media for Jackson Hewitt. Martha O'Gorman was the former Director of Communications and Partner for Lendman Advertising, before joining Jackson Hewitt. Martha remembers the magnitude of our debt, "At the end of the tax season, Jackson Hewitt owed us $300,000 that they didn't have. We put together a payment schedule, and they met every one of those payments. John did not leave one vendor or supplier holding the bag for anything. He paid them all off."

Late that fall, another friend and original investor, Paul Grunberg, agreed to loan the company $500,000 to cover most of our cash problems and make it to the next tax season. In return, the company granted him options to purchase the same amount of stock. Options for his five-month loan to Jackson Hewitt were ultimately worth 13 million dollars.

Time, loyal friends, and hard work finally alleviated the intense pressure on our company.

Always Go On the Field Planning to Win

As I look back now, I realize that this season was one of the darkest times of my career. You may relate to a time like this in your life. Even today, millions of Americans are recovering from a tumultuous economy, business failures, and bleak job prospects. During these seasons of life, the most important thing to do is to keep moving forward. Even during that awful time when the company faltered, I realized I would go on.

Since we had some profitable locations, the worst thing that could happen was the company would scale back to just 20 or 30 offices; shrink down to our smallest, successful units and build from that base. We still had the software. At the very worst, I would run one office, make the coffee, and prepare tax returns again. If that was what it took, I would have done it. Start over. I never thought about throwing in the towel; quitting was never an option. I knew that there was a cadre – a small group – who would persevere with me through this time, even if we had to take a huge step back.

In your own business, make a commitment to yourself, your employees, investors, or managers that losing is not an option. Go onto the playing field,

in sports or in business, planning to win. Vince Lombardi is quoted as saying, "It's not whether you get knocked down, it's whether you get up… Second place is meaningless. You can't always be first, but you have to believe that you should have been – that you were never beaten – that time just ran out on you."[2] If I can't win, I make sure I learn enough so that I'll have a better chance of winning next time.

A crucial lesson we learned is not to bite off more than we could chew. I know we've all heard this, but I've lived it. Take it from me; manage your growth and your cash flow. Don't over-extend because the biggest risk for entrepreneurs is stumbling, falling down, and not having the resources to get back up. We had a good niche in a great industry. I know that my friends, investors, and business partners who believed in me made all the difference in recovering from this fall.

Learn and Grow

In 1990, just one year after our struggle with Wards, Jackson Hewitt operated 230 offices–117 in Wards' stores—and had almost seven million dollars in gross volume from tax preparation. We survived the over-expansion, but we still operated like a smaller company. Mike Lepkowski, a Jackson Hewitt employee and franchisee, remembers being "confidently terrified." Mike said, "We sat around with my mom and dad and everyone was confident in John, but terrified at the growth." Before Wards, if the franchise owners needed to make changes or update the software, they would just call me up and I'd talk them through it. That had to change and we had to start acting like the big company we had become.

Some of the franchisees were not affected by our growing pains at all. These owners continued to receive the support they always had and never even realized the company was in such dire straits. My employees made me proud for making that happen and for not spreading the bad news, which might have created more problems. For many others, however, the previous year took its toll. The corporate staff struggled to overcome the financial challenges and expansion. Bill and Esther, who I hoped would help grow the company, left even though the 1990 tax season had been a success. They lost confidence in the company.

To Thine Own Self Be True

My favorite phrase from all of Shakespeare's work comes from *Hamlet*, "to thine own self be true." In business and in life, you can't please everyone all of the time, so don't try. If you're that person in your company who is liked by everyone, you have a problem. In my company, we can find dozens of people who don't like me. It's okay to always be liked if you never plan to be a leader or run your own company. You can't be everyone's friend. That doesn't get you where you want to go. You have to be tougher and challenge people. You also have to listen to their feedback because embracing your own mistakes usually begins with someone else's criticism.

Here's the hard truth for you. Not everyone can live the entrepreneurial life with its ups and downs. Not knowing whether or not our staff would receive a paycheck each month created tremendous worry and strain. Overall, we were on the verge of becoming a large company and we needed a solid plan to build both our capital and staff. That would take some faith and dusting ourselves off after this painful fall, but we were about to go into one of our greatest seasons of growth – the right way.

JOHN'S PRINCIPLES TO LIVE BY

- If it sounds too good to be true... you know the rest
- Everyone gets knocked down – winners get back up
- Don't languish over your mistakes
- When all else fails – laugh!
- Embrace criticism
- Learn by trial and error
- Always go on the field planning to win
- Mistakes are a wise person's education
- To thine own self be true

Your Challenge

How can you learn from your worst mistakes in the past to create your greatest wins for the future?

WALL STREET JOURNAL.

DITION WEDNESDAY, FEBRUARY 20, 1991 WHITE OAK, MARYLAND

ide

eace plan doesn't
nding the war.
otained privately
rms to assure the
n't be dismantled
ve Saddam Hus-
wing way out of
so said the plan
inkage" between
of the Palestinian
respond as early
proposal, which
s signs that Bush
d attack within
6 and A3)

—ned that the
much smaller
claimed, with
ng that 1.5 mil-
r involved.

D Gorbachev and
resignation.
ssion appeal, the
argest Soviet re-
s of sacrificing
rive for personal
frequent critic of
re had called for
down. In the ob-
tain argued that
ed from the cen-
separate repub-
new government
increases.
mister said that
h's, which were
est cities, have
e rate.

t conceded that
ncome taxes, af-
how to pay for
ulf war expenses.
Union plans to
its coalition part-
l temporary sur-
yments.

ents indicated that
e nation's $3.7 bil-
ent program may
is of people. Pa-
ing treatment ses-
3½ hours were up
than those with
n Page B1)

Paper and Paperboard

In millions of tons.

PAPER AND PAPERBOARD produc-
tion in the U.S. fell in December to a sea-
sonally adjusted annual rate of 79.1 million
tons from 79.5 million tons in November,
the American Paper Institute reports.

Robert Brown Finds
Riyadh Is No Place
For a War Buff

* * *

Soldier of Fortune's Editor
Sees Too Little Action,
Too Much of the Press

By TONY HORWITZ
Staff Reporter of THE WALL STREET JOURNAL

RIYADH, Saudi Arabia—Robert Brown
never met a war he didn't like. Until this
one.

The 58-year-old editor of Soldier of For-
tune magazine has seen 15 wars and insur-
gencies up close—as combatant, as corre-
spondent, and sometimes as both. He has
shrapnel in his thigh from Vietnam, and a
T-shirt that says, "I'd Rather Be Killing
Commies." The parachute bag he packed
for Saudi Arabia has in it a manual type-
writer, camera, camouflage jacket and
bulletproof vest.

But five weeks into the war, Mr. Brown
is cooling his combat boots at the Riyadh
Hyatt Regency, foiled by the U.S. mili-
tary's tight control on access to the front.
More humiliating still, he is sequestered
with a battalion of journalists, many of
whom are bewildered by the alphabet soup
of SPWs, KIAs and APCs dished out by
military spokesmen.

Dashed Expectations

"I thought I'd be riding the lead tank
into Baghdad by now," he says, spitting
snuff-juice into an empty can of alcohol-

Tax Report

A Special Summary and Forecast
Of Federal and State Tax
Developments

FAX TRAX TAX, as the IRS updates
methods of seizing unpaid taxes by levy.

In extreme cases, the IRS can collect de-
linquent bills by levying on wages, bank ac-
counts, or other assets. New guidelines say
agents may use facsimile wires, instead of
the mail, to send levy notices and cancella-
tions to employers, banks, and others that
agree to it. Financial institutions must
freeze an account for 21 days before sending
cash to the IRS; the new guidelines say in-
stitutions can't stop paying interest during a
freeze and must send it to the IRS if the bal-
ance is below the levy. Institutions may not
deduct fees from levy amounts.

The guidelines do call for some compas-
sion. Social Security, veterans', pension, and
foster-care benefits are subject to levy un-
der the law; but the guidelines note that lev-
ies would thwart the purposes of these bene-
fits. Thus, agents should consider hardship
and whether other available funds are ade-
quate to pay the delinquent taxes.

"Levy [on] these types of income only
in flagrant and aggravated cases," the
guidelines tell agents.

NOT TO WORRY: Uncle Sam is paying
refunds, despite rumors to the contrary.

Return preparers are picking up the false
reports, especially in the Southeast. Gener-
ally, customers call about filing early, be-
cause they've heard the government is trying
to divert refunds to pay for the war. There's
no truth in that, says the Treasury. The IRS
is authorizing refunds—over two million of
them, averaging $963, by Feb. 8. And the
Treasury is paying them as usual.

Tom Bloch, president of H & R Block,
says the rumor is "pretty ridiculous," but
"fairly widespread." Terry Blitz, a Block re-
gional director, says variations in Tennessee
and the Carolinas were that refunds
wouldn't be paid until June 30, or Nov. 30, on
claims filed after Feb. 28. The rumor has hit
Louisiana. And John Hewitt, president of
Jackson Hewitt Tax Service, a national
chain, says offices in Virginia and Dallas
have had inquiries about it.

SIT TIGHT, if the IRS has questioned
pension income on your 1988 return.

The IRS says it will try to resolve the ap-
parent discrepancies by itself. It sent 780,000
queries—thousands probably unnecessary—
to filers who put taxable pension or annuity
income correctly on 1988 returns, but failed
to list total pensions. The IRS needs totals
for initial computer matching of return en-

Fading Boom

Japan Feels a Squeeze
As Firms Cut Outlays
And Bankruptcies Rise

Foreign Investment Is Pared,
And Higher Interest Rates
Hit Even Sony and Nissan

But Economy Stays Resilient

By MARCUS W. BRAUCHLI
And CLAY CHANDLER
Staff Reporters of THE WALL STREET JOURNAL

TOKYO—Japan is becoming a bit more
like other industrial nations.

Much of its once-amazing financial
clout has been dissipated by higher inter-
est rates, a collapse in stock prices and jit-
ters in the real-estate market. Economic
growth is slowing. Corporate earnings are
shrinking. Bankruptcies are rising.

Japanese investors are selling U.S.
Treasury securities and New York office
towers. The wave of foreign takeovers by
Japanese companies is subsiding. And
even Japanese banks have become tight-
fisted. Many of them are borrowing heav-
ily to meet new rules requiring them to lift
their capital to about 8% of their loans.

All this is a remarkable change. For
much of the 1980s, Japan seemed unstoppa-
ble. With banks awash in cash, stocks soar-
ing and property grossly overvalued, Japa-
nese spent lavishly. They did the biggest
takeovers, the most sensational real-estate
deals, the priciest art acquisitions.

Adjustment 'Inevitable'

"Japan as a rich country was caused by
a kind of financial bubble," says Takeshi
Ohta, a director of Daiwa Bank Ltd. and a
former Bank of Japan official. "Now, some
adjustment is inevitable."

Is this the end of mighty Japan Inc.?

Hardly. The world's second-biggest
economy, though slowing, remains one of
the world's strongest. Japan's gross na-
tional product last year is estimated to
have grown more than 5%, up from 4.9%
growth in 1989 and more than double the
average in other industrialized countries.
Its capital balance is believed to have
risen 16% to $700 billion and, in absolute
terms, to have outstripped U.S. spending
by 33%.

According to government officials and
corporate executives, Japan is merely
gathering its strength for further economic

Chapter 6
Contribute to the Team

I'm a numbers person. Arithmetic, taxes… even writing code wasn't hard for me. Teams and people, in general, are much more complex to manage and I have yet to meet one person - one franchisee - who will follow our system exactly. They all think they know better. Never mind that I have 46 years in the business and a wealth of knowledge from working with thousands of franchisees. They forget that I've experienced incredible growth and success, skated on the edge of bankruptcy, and come back as the fastest growing tax industry franchise system developer in the U.S. They all feel like they know better. They will either learn or fail.

It's Up to You

Still, I try to get my message across. I mentioned in this book's dedication that I have a fanatical need to give to every human being I meet more than they give to me. The exception is my parents, of course, who I will never catch. These days, in order to consistently give to my team at Liberty, I personally invest my life and time into my employees and franchise owners. Once a week, I meet with our corporate team to challenge ourselves, challenge each other, and break boundaries as we strive to improve. On average, every other day during tax season I hold conference calls for all of our franchisees to help them set the standard in their communities, increase profitability and, most importantly, create raving fans through second-to-none customer service. The last point deserves its own chapter later.

What it Takes to Become a Millionaire

In one corporate meeting, we talked about a specific goal: becoming a millionaire. We agreed that most people would love to reach this goal, but the vast majority will not get there. Why? What's the main reason they won't see seven figures on their personal financial statement? I told my team, and I'm telling you, that the number one reason you will or will not reach this goal is YOU. Every day, you hold yourself back or propel yourself forward. Becoming a

millionaire is all about your commitment – how badly do you want it? If you want it, you'll get it, but you must persevere.

Remember, most people in life try to make you ordinary – to bring you back to normal or average. Peer pressure is the best example of this. The worst insult you can give me is to say, "You remind me of someone else." Most people settle for ordinary. To be extraordinary, join or create a winning team and contribute to that team as if your life and your dreams depend on it. They do. A small percentage of the population becomes rich and it's not a magic formula. Hundreds of books have been written about it. Let me make it simple for you: *find something you like to do, work hard, and persevere.*

Perseverance Pays

In the early 1990s, our perseverance paid off. Jackson Hewitt's brand recognition and public awareness of the franchise opportunities grew. *Entrepreneur, Success Magazine*, and other publications consistently recognized the company as one of the fastest growing, top companies in the country. Major newspapers like the *Los Angeles Times* and *USA Today* featured Jackson Hewitt as one of the country's top tax preparation firms.

I was ecstatic to get Jackson Hewitt's name into *Barron's*, my favorite financial newspaper, and *The Wall Street Journal*. I had tried several times to get into *The Wall Street Journal's* tax column that ran on Wednesday's front page. At Jackson Hewitt, we sent *The Wall Street Journal* a press release almost every week. I finally met with a *Wall Street Journal* writer who wrote a front-page article. That opened up other doors - I began appearing on national television programs such as CNN's *Your Money* and NBC's *Dateline*. This was definitely a stretch for a guy who doesn't even like public speaking. I'm an introvert and this was way outside of my comfort zone. Our hard work was finally paying off and people were taking notice.

Stay Ahead of the Trends

This success didn't just happen. Again, it was perseverance, foresight, and some developments in our industry that I knew were game changers. Plus, in the late 1980s the government made extensive changes to the tax code. The result: confusion – kind of like today. People needed more help than ever with their tax preparation.

Refund anticipation loans (RALS), came into play with banks giving customers short-term loans based on their anticipated refund amount from the IRS. Taxpayers had checks in hand within three days (and eventually one day, as the IRS sped up the process) instead of two to three weeks, if they waited for their refund. For as long as I've done taxes, there has always been a percentage of the population that wants the benefit of their tax refund as fast as possible and is willing to pay a fee for it. This is the biggest check that they see all year long.

Half of this country lives paycheck to paycheck. They don't have savings and when there's an emergency, like their car breaks down, or a major catastrophe, like a fire or a serious illness, they don't have any money to handle the situation. They are in danger of not being able to pay their rent, utilities, and other daily expenses.

We found that some people overspent at Christmas – even using their January rent money for gifts – and they would catch up with their refund. It caused some people to look for this help from paid preparers, instead of doing it themselves because they could get their money faster.

It didn't take a rocket scientist or, in my case, a tax expert to see that demand for these services would continue to skyrocket in the coming years. The difference was we had an edge. As with electronic filing, Jackson Hewitt had a technological advantage. We could easily adapt our computerized system to communicate with the lending banks. Our product was more accurate than other firms who still prepared returns by hand. Fewer errors and a faster process meant smoother customer service experiences in the offices.

Free Is Not Your Usual Four-Letter Word

Along with this new system, I added a new word to our vocabulary: free! I had no idea that this four-letter word would cause such a stir. I decided that Jackson Hewitt would offer free electronic filing to our customers. Of all the decisions I made over the years, this is one that people fought the most. Most electronic filers and even some of my own franchisees and staff thought it was crazy to give away something for which we previously had charged. After all, they argued, customers expected to pay for it.

Fortunately, the IRS also backed me. "The situation was ripe for someone to make an impact," said Lenny Holt, with the IRS. "There were a couple of half-hearted attempts at it, but John was the guy who had a plan and made it

happen. I was a little surprised at how quickly he grew the company, but not surprised that he was the guy who did it. Faster than any company of any size, he saw the wisdom of making electronic filing the way you do business. John realized you could attract a lot of business, gain some notoriety, and–oh by the way–stay in the good graces of the IRS if you actively and enthusiastically participated in electronic filing at no cost to the customer. He was the right person, at the right place, at the right time...."

In tax season 1991, all 320 Jackson Hewitt offices began aggressively advertising free electronic filing.

The Formula for a Winning Team

Like I said, I'm a numbers guy. Creating systems comes naturally to me. Unfortunately, managing people isn't always as neat and structured as writing computer software or doing a tax return, but I have learned some factors that equate to a winning team.

You Can't Teach Attitude

I mentioned this earlier and it's worth writing again - to me, attitude is everything. This is the number one attribute I looked for at Jackson Hewitt, and continues to be number one at Liberty Tax today. We can teach people how to run their business, how to market it, and support them with tax and technical knowledge. We can help them get capital to set up their business. What we can't teach is attitude; the positive, team-focused, customer service attitude that separates winners from losers. I don't mean we have to recruit always happy, yes-people either; part of success and being a winner is doing what you say, not just spouting the right lines.

People will try to fool you during interviews. Nobody will show you that they have a bad attitude if they are trying to get a job. As an introvert, I am very observant and I ask probing questions to see beyond the mask. For example, I ask them for references of people who reported to them, not the other way around. I ask them to describe their best supervisors and what attributes made them so successful. If they have worked in a franchise organization, I ask for references of franchisees that dealt with them.

The toughest step is when you find someone who doesn't fit and moving him or her out. Just as people can make a great culture, principle violators can also create a bad culture. Jack Welch, chairman and CEO of General Electric from 1981 to 2001, described four categories of managers. Type 1 shares your values and performs well. For them the sky's the limit. Type 2 shares your values, but misses the numbers. He recommends giving them another chance or two. Type 3 doesn't share your values or perform well. In this case, it's a no-brainer — get rid of them. My strategy is to tell them that they need to go find another place to be extraordinary.

Welch maintains that Type 4 is the toughest call of all: the person who doesn't share the values, but delivers the numbers. This type is the toughest to part with because organizations always want to deliver and to let someone go who gets the job done is yet another unnatural act. But we have to remove these Type 4s because they have the power, by themselves, to destroy the open, informal, trust-based culture we need to win today and tomorrow.[3] You can teach job skills, but you can't teach attitude. This is a very tough call for me because I tend to want to live with high-performance people because their results are so good. One of my weaknesses is that I'm too forgiving of people. I don't pull the trigger fast enough. Plus, I do remember one lesson from school. President Lincoln took a chance on Ulysses S. Grant because of his excellent performance leading the Union Army to victory at Vicksburg in 1863. That's despite his reputation as an alcoholic a decade earlier, when he was asked to resign from the Army.[4] The rest, as they say, is history.

Be Part of a Bigger Vision

Even now, I look for potential owners who want to be part of a bigger vision: to change people's lives. Most franchise organizations focus on recruiting franchisees with investment capital. I'm more interested in the team and creating a culture to help others succeed. We called our franchisees "business partners," and I still fully embrace that philosophy today. Many of our first franchisees were beginning to net a great deal of money. Other franchisees were realizing their dreams of owning a business, regardless of their background.

I loved to brag about my successful business partners—still do. People like Vicki Lemon. Vicki, a mother and part-time tax preparer when she joined Jackson Hewitt, opened one store in Gloucester, Virginia. The first year, she prepared about 300 returns. During the summer, for a reduction of rent, she

worked for the landlord of the strip center where her office was located. Each year, following our marketing advice, she grew the business until it was worth $300,000 and processed almost 2000 returns per year. That's better than an average H&R Block location in many larger markets. The successes of the franchisees energized me. I realized then that it was not only the competition—the drive to be as big as H&R Block—that inspired me. Knowing that I had a hand in making peoples lives better probably inspired me the most.

A BIGGER VISION

"John offered franchisees a chance to make their own personal mark in life. Not only the opportunity to make some money, but to learn business skills, to work within a system, and to have gratification. Jackson Hewitt's business philosophy was different than other franchises, because it was built a lot more on a relationship-oriented service and not a submarine sandwich or a donut. It's more intangible. There's a fulfillment from helping people with their taxes/finances that's very unique to this business. People can make money from three different sources: as an employee, as an owner of a franchise, or from owning equity in the company. John offered people all three, and the energy and momentum was tremendous...." - **Gordon D'Angelo, *Jackson Hewitt Initial Investor and Executive, Founder of NEXT Financial***

Delegation is Key for Your Success

My biggest challenge during this growth phase was me. To survive as a national competitor, I was forced to address some of my own issues including my growth and development as a CEO, and building a corporate team to support the influx of franchisees.

For the three years following the Wards' contract, I promoted and added key personnel to develop badly needed departments: communications, legal, and human resources, for example. Up to the 1991 tax season, Linda and I,

with a handful of managers and staff, did everything. We had titles, but it was a very informal specialization, and we often jumped in to help regardless of departments or responsibilities. I had to make a personal change. I could no longer make every decision, or be a part of every meeting and conference call. I had to select and lead the people who would make the decisions. This was not an easy switch for a hands-on person like me.

Share Power and Knowledge

Today, part of Liberty's basic training for all franchisees and employees includes a seminar on delegation, one of the biggest problems in business. I'm not alone in my struggle with this part of management; in fact, this can be the number one challenge for new CEOs. Why? Lack of trust and the feeling that no one can do this job as well as you can.

One of my weaknesses is being controlling and I have to fight that because it's necessary for people to make mistakes. If I went around and corrected everyone's mistakes on one day, that day would be better, but the next day would be worse because there would be no improvement. I had to learn to let people make mistakes so they would get better at their jobs in the future. A principle to which I adhere is if a person is going to make a mistake that doesn't risk severely injuring or crippling the company, I go ahead and let them make that mistake. If it's a do-or-die situation for the company, I step in. You can't let them make that kind of mistake. You have to intercede.

I've learned the hard way that giving power away doesn't mean that you have less power; it means that you have more. If you are going to rise to power, you must have people who report to you. Great leaders have followers who are also leaders. You want to become the chief of chiefs. It's a big step up to manage chiefs instead of just managing employees. The word delegate is a verb. It means appointing others daily to act as your company's representative and carry out responsibilities that take you away from your main focus: acting like a CEO. This is a skill that we have to practice and the sooner you master it, the more successful you'll become.

Walt Ewell, our CFO at the time, remembers the early days riding on the edge of bankruptcy and how we had gotten along with little or nothing to build Jackson Hewitt. He knows that I prided myself on operating on a shoestring budget and initially had a hard time letting go of that. Walt said, "When I joined Jackson Hewitt, if you had to mail something you had to

go to John Hewitt. He'd pull out the drawer of this big schoolteacher's desk. He had sheets of stamps. I don't know how many stamps he had, but he'd be ripping them out—counting them out. We're trying to do a direct mail campaign to California of 10,000 pieces and we'd have everyone in the office sitting around licking stamps and doing the mailing. I told him we really needed a postage meter. I mean, I know it cost money, but... I got there right in that transition period from a small operation to a large company, and at times it was difficult."

Hire Others Who See the Big Picture

Hiring and allocating managers the right way challenged me. The company was doing well, but still operating on a barebones budget, with not a great deal of money available for large salaries, impressive office space, or great benefit packages. An interviewee who became our legal counsel and director of tax and software almost didn't come for the interview when she saw the building. Kathleen Curry remembers, "The office was in this industrial area, way in the back, run-down... I'd been interviewing with law firms. But the person I interviewed with was fabulous, as enthusiastic as the day is long about the company. I started in September. By January, I was in charge of the legal department." Kathleen was able to look past the run-down building and grasp the vision for what we were doing. She saw the big picture.

All I could offer managers and employees was opportunity—a chance to be part of the vision and, for the right people, promotions earlier in their careers than would have been possible at a larger, more structured company.

Hire for Strengths

In growing my company, again, first I hire for attitude; then I clearly define the skill I wanted to achieve and then looked for the right person with those strengths. Sue Ventresca, our manager in New York, was promoted to Director of Field Operations. My daughter, Patti, who graduated from college with a marketing degree, joined the company as Director of Human Resources and Training. I hired Martha O'Gorman as Director of Communications. She was a partner with the advertising agency to whom we owed so much money in 1989. Martha liked Jackson Hewitt, despite the risk of bankruptcy, because of the warmth, drive, and dynamics of the people. As with the franchisees, we hired employees with the right attitude. It's hard to measure the benefits of

hiring for attitude, but positive attitudes are contagious. The culture of "can-do" and "success" attracted Martha and other managers to take a chance and become part of this upstart company.

The other thing I offered was ownership of what they were helping to build. We granted stock options to every year-round employee, from the regional directors to the receptionists. The first options cost $10 per share. If an employee bought just 100 of those options and held them, their realized gain when Jackson Hewitt sold in 1997 was $139,000.

Hire People Who Know Something You Don't

If you're a smart and capable entrepreneur, you know how hard it can be to admit that others may be smarter than you in certain areas. Dan Grunburg, our board member Paul's son, had already opened eight stores in Boston when the IRS allowed electronic filing there in 1989. A Ph.D. graduate of Massachusetts Institute of Technology, Dan's forte was computer science and engineering. He told me that the Apple systems and program that Jackson Hewitt used were "rinky-dink" compared to what was new in the marketplace and just didn't make the cut for a national company.

Dan proposed that he and several associates rework the program to improve its capabilities, change to an IBM compatible program and, overall, make it more user friendly. I accepted his proposal and later hired Dan to head up the technology department. Look for people who are experts in their field, delegate, and trust them to do their job. Monitoring for results comes next – we'll get to that.

Growth Also Brings Growing Pains

The growth of the corporate staff was necessary, but difficult for some original staff members. Linda had a hard time. She left the company at my request in 1992. It was a hard decision to ask Linda to step down; she played a big part in Jackson Hewitt's early success. To this day, we can't agree on exactly what happened and we don't dredge up the past.

Growth meant growing pains, but this time we had learned to manage the opportunities and losses along the way. By 1992, we appeared on the *INC. 500* listing as one of the fastest growing private companies. Jackson Hewitt was reported to be one of the country's top tax preparation firms. The accolades and recognition were coming in faster than even I expected. All of

this publicity and the company's fantastic results meant something else. The problem that had plagued us from the beginning —raising capital—became easier. That would lead to both a blessing and the turn of events that cost me the company that bears my name.

JOHN'S PRINCIPLES TO LIVE BY

- Contribute to the team – it's up to you
- What it takes to be a millionaire: your commitment
- Perseverance pays
- Stay ahead of the trends
- Winners do what others won't
- The formula for a winning team – you can't teach attitude
- Be part of a bigger vision
- Delegation is key for your success
- Share power and knowledge
- Hire others who see the big picture
- Hire for strengths
- Hire people who know something you don't
- Growth also brings growing pains

Your Challenge

How can you contribute to your team in a different
way to achieve different results?

Business

CLASSIFIED

JACKSON HEWITT
TAX SERVICE

NO. 2 TAX SERVICE IS TOPS IN GROWTH

Jackson Hewitt has been one of the nation's fastest-growing private companies over the past decade. Since John and Linda Hewitt and 11 other investors bought the former Mel Jackson's Tax Service in 1982, the number of tax offices has grown every year but one.

The company has prospered, in large part, because it has ridden the electronic wave sweeping across tax preparation. It's so good at electronic filing that the IRS hires it to write the test all tax services must pass in order to file returns by computer.

John Hewitt, the driving force of a company that's shaking things up on H&R's block.

REVENUES
in millions of dollars

PROFIT

NUMBER OF TAX OFFICES

RETURNS FILED ELECTRONICALLY
in thousands

JOHN EARLE/Staff ; CHARLIE MEADS/Photo

SOURCE: The company

By Dave Mayfield
Staff writer

Five years ago, when a whippersnapper by the name of John Hewitt was just beginning to make some noise in the tax business, a Washington Post reporter asked H&R Block Chairman Henry Bloch what he thought of the young upstart.

"I don't think I've heard of Hewitt," Bloch said.

More than 860 offices later, Jackson Hewitt Inc., the Virginia Beach-based tax service, is still a distant second to Block in the tax-preparation game.

But you won't catch Block executives simply dismissing their competitor any longer.

"You can't help but notice them," says Harry W. Buckley, president of H&R Tax Services.

It has been 11 years since John Hewitt, college dropout, computer whiz and ex-H&R Block manager, gathered together a dozen investors to buy the six offices of a rickety tax service in Hampton Roads called Mel Jackson's.

He nearly bankrupted the company once during his aggressive expansion of it. But in recent years, as Hewitt matured from an awkward entrepreneur to a sure-handed professional manager, the company has settled into a fairly steady upward groove.

Maturing of founder and firm

John Hewitt doesn't brag about Jackson Hewitt Inc. like he used to, but he doesn't need to. The company's results talk for him: rapid expansion, satisfied franchisees and, this month, publicly traded stock.

Indeed, there's a feeling among Jackson Hewitt executives and its 400 franchisees across the country that their company is finally starting to arrive.

Jackson Hewitt expects to begin the next season in January with a record 900 offices in 37 states. That's up from 614 offices in 29 states last season.

It's made all kinds of magazine "best" lists in 1993. 18th-best franchiser, according to Success magazine. 60th best franchise, according to Entrepreneur; one of Inc. magazine's 500 fastest-growing private companies.

It's just moved into a new 24,000-square-foot headquarters on Bonney Road, off the Virginia Beach Norfolk Expressway.

And now, within the next week or so, the company plans to go public by listing its stock on the national over-the-counter trading system. Based on recent private trades of about $12 a share, Jackson Hewitt roughly 5 million shares will have a market value of about $60 million. There are 700 shareholders.

The 44-year-old Hewitt, president of the company, said in an interview last week that managing growth will be his biggest challenge.

"We have to be careful that we don't overstep, that we don't go into a giant stumble," he says, adding "

Please see **HEWITT**, *Page E*

Please see HEWITT, Page E

Chapter 7
Monitor Results, Not Activities

In business, first it's about principles, and then it's all about results. "Monitor results, not activities" is one of my core teachings at Liberty Tax and it extends to my family. It also led to a great strategy I learned when raising my son, Danny. Say "no" by saying "yes."

In high school, Danny was 5'10" and only weighed about 130 pounds. This skinny kid decided he wanted to play football and his mother, Linda, was livid. The thought of him getting tackled by players who weighed 250 to 300 pounds nearly sent her over the edge. Here I was, stuck in the middle. While I am a big believer in tough love, as a Dad, I do have a soft side and I didn't want to always say "no" to Danny. Even as a parent, I was looking for a win-win.

I went to Danny and set it up in advance, so I wouldn't tip my hand. Before I ever mentioned football I said, "If you wanted to make Honor Roll, could you?" Mr. Cocky said, "Yes, of course." I said, "I'll make you a deal - if you make the Honor Roll, then you can play football." Danny was a B/C student, so based on previous results I was off the hook.

I had to trick Danny. That's how you become blameless. In negotiations, you make them say in advance what they are going to do and when they don't do it, it's their own fault. It was too late – Danny couldn't back away from the deal that came out of his own mouth. Here's where the trick really got good: football practice starts in the summer, so Danny had to make Honor Roll back in April to get to join the football team in July and August. If he was going to play football, he had to think at least four months ahead of time and consistently produce great results in school. I had said "yes," based on results and now it was all on him. It had nothing to do with me; I was the good guy. Danny dug his own grave, which wouldn't be anywhere near a football field.

Well, Danny never did make Honor Roll, but he did go on to play All-City volleyball for two years; a much better sport for a 130-pound kid and, as a side benefit, his mother was happy. Win-win-win – a negotiating strategy based on results. Learn to say "no" by saying "yes."

Live the Mission Every Day

Based on results, we were at the top of our game. Expectations were high for our company and in November of 1993, I told a reporter from the *Virginian-Pilot and Ledger Star,* "As of today, we finally have the capital and management in place for the foreseeable future." And we did – then. In the same article, Paul Littman, a franchise owner and former company employee said, "John has matured wonderfully over the last five years. He's become a major-league manager, really risen to the position."

In 1993, we declared "Winning Customers for Life," the mission of our company. With the help of a franchise consulting company, Management 2000, we developed our guiding principles. I visualized a company where a mission statement meant more than just a few words on an annual report. "Winning Customers for Life" would be our motivation. I had our mission statement and principles printed on pads of paper and distributed them to every office and employee. When anyone saw either a breach of our principles or a great example of them, they were to fill out a "Mission Moment" and give it to the person involved. Sometimes it worked, sometimes it didn't, but it got people talking and thinking about how to live the mission everyday. The truth is a happy customer with a check in hand quickly is the best measure of a mission.

The company gained more recognition in January of 1994 when the stock began trading on the National Association of Securities Dealers' (NASDAQ) national market system. Jackson Hewitt went public in an unusual way, by converting existing shares instead of issuing new ones. We didn't gain any cash by going public, but now analysts would take notice of Jackson Hewitt and the current shares were more liquid. The market value of the company on the first day of trading reached $44 million.

Topping off all of the exciting events and goodwill surrounding the company, the 1994 tax season was a banner year. The company opened 264 new offices for a total of 878 and electronically filed over a half-million tax returns. For the first time ever, our solid balance sheet brought money to us. Creditors and vendors began to seek us out. The banker who initially worked with Linda and me to get our first Small Business Administration loan called.

She said, "What would it take to get your business?"

These are words I had never heard before from creditors, and I didn't hesitate in asking for what we needed. "We want an operating line of credit equal to the one we have now ($3 million), plus a $2.5 million dollar line of credit that we can loan to our franchisees for expansion." The bank agreed. As a guarantor, we loaned the entire $2.5 million to existing franchisees to open additional stores. Sales of new territories hit a record high.

It wasn't just banks taking note of us. Before we went public, in the summer of 1993, Jackson Hewitt solicited and received several bids from venture capitalists. I supported this plan to complete our expansion and pay salaries for an expanded field operations staff, now headed by Jack Seal, a former franchisee. The board voted to approve a $3 million sale of preferred stock to three venture capital funds managed by Geo Capital Partners. For their investment in the company, Geo Capital Partners gained a seat on Jackson Hewitt's Board of Directors and equity of about 10% of the company.

Inspect Your Expectations

The money flowed in and the expansion continued. In the fall of 1994, we penned a deal with Walmart to open tax offices and Copy, Pack and Ship stores in 18 Walmart locations across the country. With both sales and expansion up, we expected to start the 1995 tax season with 300-350 additional locations. Operating now in the nation's number one retailer, our possibilities for the future seemed endless and we looked for other partners to continue our growth.

Now is a good time for a reality check. Inspect your expectations. This is a difficult lesson, because I'm all about reaching for the impossible. When a negative person comes into my office and tells me that they're simply a "realist," I want to grab them and shake them and change them. I have this seriously fanatical goal to improve everyone I meet, even though I know I can't. Being a realist gets you nowhere! If you're facing a life of realism, you're facing a boring future. Remember, if you act normal you will only get normal results. A word of caution, reaching for the extraordinary will never be easy. We've all heard about the road less traveled; how many of us are really willing to walk it? Choosing to be exceptional brings challenges. This is why I tell all of my

franchise owners to listen to me. I've been through the best and worst seasons of business.

Describing 1995 as the worst year for our industry would be the understatement of the century. It was one hundred times worse than anything we had ever experienced. We were hit with a huge catastrophe, courtesy of the IRS. In your business, there will be challenges, both within and out of your control, which you have to learn to navigate. Again, God doesn't put anyone on this earth to just skate through. We're supposed to face adversity – it's part of God's system to build character and test us. Without any downtimes, we wouldn't appreciate the uptimes as much. While this is obvious to me today, it was of little consolation in 1995.

Cut Your Losses Quickly

The last thing you need is a lesson on tax history here – I'll spare you. But to make a complicated situation easier to understand, let me give you the basics. Lloyd Bentsen, head of the U.S. Treasury Department, announced some changes to stop fraud surrounding electronic filing and refund anticipation loans. This affected how and when taxpayers and preparers were paid. "Certain people inside the IRS became convinced that electronic filing, and particularly the refund anticipation loans, were creating fraud by attracting fraud and scam promoters," said Lenny Holt, a former director of operations and marketing with the IRS. "In my humble opinion, they were mistaken. I used to argue, with some degree of success, that electronic filing and bank products simply made it easier to detect fraud. You have so many people looking and checking with automated systems and specified criteria—the preparer, the banks, the IRS—returns could come into the IRS service centers by the billions and each one could be checked." Without getting too technical, there are two parts to a refund for many customers: overpayment of federal withholding and the Earned Income Tax Credit (EITC). At that time, the IRS system was set up so they could only send one deposit into a bank account, the first part of the refund. For example, some people who anticipated $2,000-4,000 direct deposits only received $10-20 because of the IRS holds. The IRS could then hold the rest of the refund for two months or more, waiting clearance. Then it

was mailed directly to the taxpayer, completely circumventing tax preparation firms and the banks that had issued loans.

If these IRS rules confuse you, think about how millions of taxpayers felt. They wondered what had happened to their money. Customers refused to come in and pay their tax preparation fees after getting what they perceived to be such poor, slow service from tax offices. The franchisees weren't paid, so in turn they could not pay royalties to the corporate office, make payments on outstanding promissory notes or, in some cases, pay employees. We immediately stopped making loans.

SAVING THE COMPANY - AGAIN

"John knew. He knew each day of the tax season how things were going. He could sense the momentum. When the first check came through from the IRS, John said, 'this isn't enough money, it's not right. We don't know enough about this. We can't make these loans.' He stopped it right away. It took H&R Block two weeks to stop it. John saved the company from loaning large amounts of money to customers who couldn't pay them back. It could have been much worse."
- **John Paris, *former Counsel to Jackson Hewitt***

Create a Strategy for Damage Control

The confusion soon turned into violence. Many low-income families needed their money – relied on it every year. The new process frustrated and angered customers at all tax preparation offices and caused some who needed the money to pay rent and buy food to become desperate. We had bomb threats and fistfights in our franchises. The tax code was formed in 1913 and nothing like this had ever happened.

"It was a terrible time for our franchisees," remembers Jack Seal, a former franchisee and director of field operations. "They couldn't help the customers. Someone pulled a gun on our franchisee in Salisbury. He took the customer to his bank and wrote the person a check out of his own account. After that,

he gave up his franchise… he didn't want to be involved. Kathy Dusza was managing offices in Houston and a customer punched her. Up in Rochester, a disgruntled customer threw hot coffee on one of the preparers. It was a bad scene all around."

Some franchisees were forced out of business because they took such a financial beating. We negotiated the line of credit for the franchisees at just the wrong time. Essentially, we got spanked again for aggressive expansion. In any normal year, our expansion would have been fantastic; this was a 1 out of 1,000 catastrophic chance. It didn't matter that the disaster resulted from choices made within the IRS, not because of decisions made by us. I took little consolation in that.

Keep Persevering During the Storm

Jackson Hewitt and other companies in the tax preparation and lending business made several attempts to influence the IRS, but it seemed that nothing worked. An unlikely ally came to our defense: the news media. The only way we solved our customer service problems was to go to the major newspapers and tell our story. When the articles were published, we blew them up as posters and put them around the offices, including on the windows. When people came in to complain, they could read the truth. It took a couple of weeks to get our story into the media and post articles, and it did solve our problem with customer service. The threats stopped.

The Business Newspaper for the Tax and Accounting Community

Vol.9 No.2 January 16-February 5, 1995

ACCOUNTINGTODAY

THE 1995 TAX SEASON

Jackson Hewitt works around RAL crackdown

by Sandy Hock

VIRGINIA BEACH, VA. — Jackson Hewitt Tax Service's 1995 refund anticipation loan business is poised to be a paradox: painful, yet potentially prolific.

The U.S. Treasury Department's elimination of the direct deposit indicator, an Internal Revenue Service procedure that notified electronic filers of expected refunds, turned the company's RAL business on its head late last year. Banks use the DDI as a signal that the loans will be made safely.

The good news: Jackson Hewitt found three new banks — Chemical Bank, Bank One and Beneficial National Bank — to back its RAL program. The bad news: The loan requirements have become stricter.

The tougher standards will disqualify about 20 percent of the company's clientele, said spokeswoman Martha O'Gorman.

For instance, customers who weren't primary filers last year will not be accepted as RAL clients. A lien against a consumer for student loan payments also nixes a chance at a RAL.

The company plans to warn customers about the new stringent loan process. Jackson Hewitt, with 1,200 U.S. locations, will distribute a brochure that lays out the procedure.

"The problem is people get used to having a service," O'Gorman said. "To take it away with really no explanation is going to cause problems."

The warning comes because once electronic filing paperwork is filed with the IRS, a direct deposit account is established at a participating bank. Even if a bank decides not to grant the RAL, the refund must be deposited in the designated account, O'Gorman said.

Customers still will receive quicker refunds under this "accelerated check" scenario. But only because they won't go through the mail; refunds will be directly deposited into their accounts.

Jackson Hewitt also will take a hit when a customer drops from RAL to accelerated check status. Instead of the $29 to $100 fee the company receives from the bank for a RAL, it will get $15 to $25 for an accelerated check refund.

Jackson Hewitt's RAL fees reached almost $4 million, or 21 percent of its $18.6 million total revenue for the fiscal year ended April 30, 1994. In fiscal 1993, the company's $1.1 million fee total was 10 percent of Jackson Hewitt's 10.8 million in total revenue.

The company couldn't predict what this year's fees will be, O'Gorman said. But in a recent quarterly statement, Jackson Hewitt warned that its inability to repeat the RAL success of previous years "could materially impact the company's earnings in fiscal 1995."

Even with that announcement and its expected dip in the percentage of qualified RAL participants, the company is cautiously predicting that more RAL clients will come its way.

"A lot of the smaller tax businesses are not offering RALs this year and they'll send those wanting RALs this way," said O'Gorman, who said the new DDI rules hit small practitioners hardest. "We can't make predictions, but we see it as being very helpful for our business. I can say publicly that the big players in the industry will do better."

But H&R Block, the tax game's biggest player, predicted that the "more stringent credit criteria" it has to adopt will result in "substantially fewer RAL customers." The Kansas City, Mo.-based tax giant's stock took a 17 percent nose dive to $33.50 after the announcement.

No huge drop was seen in Jackson Hewitt's stock following its 10-Q statement last month, although it was trading at $8.25 a share early this month, just 75 cents above its 52-week low of $7.50. Its high for the past year has been $17.25.

In February of 1995, Beneficial Bank filed a lawsuit against the IRS, insisting that they allow more than one direct deposit into a bank account. This helped speed up the process again. Tax professionals, business owners, and employees in the industry flooded congressional offices with calls, faxes, and letters. While this campaign gained some support on Capitol Hill, none of these efforts saved the tax season.

Remember Your "Fight or Die Trying" Attitude

The uproar from the industry was so great that the Senate held hearings on the matter in April, 1995. Dan Grunberg, Jackson Hewitt's Director of Technology and member of the Board of Directors, among others, testified on behalf of the tax industry.

"Our side was that the IRS was unfairly beating on these lower income people who were expecting a $2000 check so that they wouldn't be evicted or so that they could buy birthday presents, or whatever," said Dan. "And the IRS, without warning, took their money away from them, and on top of that told them, 'The preparers have your money. Go get it from them'. It was an aggressive position. I was sure I was going to be audited for the rest of my life. But the Senate committee seemed pretty sympathetic. I don't think my testifying did anyone a bit of good, but it made employees and franchisees feel better. We had a chance to say our piece."

As it stood, our next step was damage control and regaining our financial footing. I scrambled to appease NationsBank[5], which held both the operating and franchisee expansion lines of credit. In June, we worked with the bank, showed them a fourteen point plan that included retrieving payments from franchisees electronically and addressing problems so they wouldn't happen again. The bank declined extending our payments or issuing us more credit.

It got worse. That same month, Jackson Hewitt's auditors included a "going concern" paragraph in their report accompanying our yearly financial statements. The auditors indicated that unless we raised additional short-term capital, there was "substantial doubt" that the company would remain in business. By law, that information must be included in the franchise-offering circular, the document sent to potential franchisees. Talk about a morale killer.

Manage Expectations and Communication

The auditor's doubt seeped into the sales staff. The director of franchise sales told them about our dire straits and questioned the company's ability to pay commissions. Melissa Salyer, a franchise sales representative, came to me.

"You have to talk to us…we're depressed," she said. I took several key members of the sales staff out to dinner and promised them that they would be paid no matter what. The money they brought in kept us alive throughout the summer.

Nancy Sutton Cunningham was our former regional director and she remembers 1995 like it was yesterday. "The franchisees had lots of personal loss. Many used their life savings, but still had debts to the company. We worked with them to get their obligations paid," said Nancy. "We put people on payment and action plans, sorting out with them what needed to be paid and what could wait. We tried to find alternatives for them, and worked with their banks. The big unknown was the IRS."

We needed money but the IRS situation made it difficult to raise funds. Investors didn't understand enough about the IRS to know whether or not this would be a continuing policy or just an anomaly, a one-time event. I waived my salary completely. Most of the managers took 20% pay cuts. We didn't layoff any non-seasonal workers and never asked the support staff to take pay cuts—many of them couldn't afford it. At the same time, we tried to keep the franchisees alive. Our company lost 15-20% of its franchisees, but the rest hung on, doing what they needed to do to get to the following tax season and pay their debts. Plus, the IRS had committed that refunds coded for satisfying bank loans would, indeed, go to the banks. In return, Beneficial dropped their lawsuit against the IRS. The industry planned a full recovery next tax season.

Still, I needed to raise money and do it quickly. Like Nancy, I thought the biggest problem would be the IRS and convincing investors that sweeping changes wouldn't happen again. The real question became who would lead our company? The culture was changing. Were we still in the business of being number one and "Winning Customers for Life," or were we now simply building a business to sell, so that someone else could take care of our customers?

Be a Fanatical Entrepreneur

For many of my franchisees, working with me is getting a crash course in what it means to be an entrepreneur. An entrepreneur has a fairly accurate vision of the future and is extremely committed to his/her business, customers, and employees. An entrepreneur gives loyalty and receives it in return. An entrepreneur plays in the game of business the way my son's teammate, Julio, played on the basketball court.

During this time, I was called "too much of an entrepreneur." I was too bold and a risk-taker. It was an easy argument to make because this describes a pure entrepreneur. I'm guilty! In fighting for my company, I was called aggressive and cocky. Guilty and guilty again! Today, I know these are the traits of a successful entrepreneur – *a fanatical entrepreneur* – win or die trying.

The company was so cash poor that if we couldn't raise capital by the end of September our only choice was massive layoffs. Two other options became available: NationsBank approved a loan in exchange for warrants (the right to buy stock) on 10% of Jackson Hewitt or Edison Venture Capital offered to buy the company at $3 per share. Our company sold for $3 per share!? Not on my watch; the company was worth so much more. To put this in perspective, approximately 24 months later Jackson Hewitt would be sold for $68 per share, but I'm getting ahead of myself. Winners do that – we remember the big win.

To keep the peace, secure the bank deal, and save the company from being sold for $3 dollars per share, I agreed to resign as CEO after the 1996 tax season, but would continue on as Chairman of the Board. I knew I had to stay through the following tax season for the sake of the franchisees. I wanted to follow through, to direct the company to next season and make sure it recovered.

If You're Not Monitoring, It's Not Happening

As I look back on 1995, I felt like we were reliving the Montgomery Ward debacle, only this time on a much larger scale. The company limped to the end of tax season without much money and with plenty of bills. I know that while most of our challenges were out of our control, if we hadn't tracked our results and made strategic changes everyday – given what we could control – 1995 would have been our last season.

Everyday, we were on it. Everyday, we ran the numbers. Everyday, we monitored what was working and what wasn't. This has become another one of my core philosophies for succeeding in business: monitor results, not activities. That year, you can bet there was a lot of activity going on. Instead, I focused on results; what worked to save our company.

As the CEO of your own company, know this: if you're not monitoring, it's not happening. Stay on it, every day. Harsh as it seems, this is a time to "trust no man." In your business, focus on results not activities. That focus saved our company.

JOHN'S PRINCIPLES TO LIVE BY

- Monitor results, not activities
- Inspect your expectations
- Cut your losses quickly
- Create a strategy for damage control
- Keep persevering during the storm
- Remember your fight or die trying attitude
- Dive into damage control
- Manage expectations and communication
- Be a fanatical entrepreneur
- If you're not monitoring, it's not happening

Your Challenge

What is your new strategy to monitor by results, not activities and when do you plan to implement it?

Part Three: Have Some Fun

My first birthday. I looked just like the Gerber baby!

My brother, Doug,
and me in the spring of 1954.

Just before high school graduation on 6/25/1967,
with my mom and sister, Ellen.

I can't understand why an H&R Block regional director didn't like my hair?

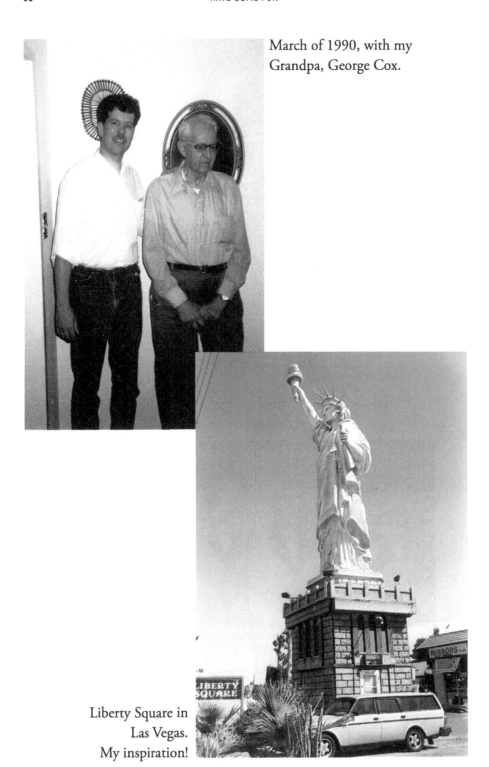

March of 1990, with my
Grandpa, George Cox.

Liberty Square in
Las Vegas.
My inspiration!

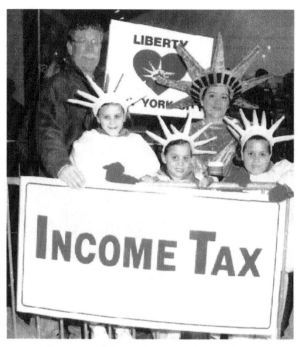

Our first crowd appearance at the Today Show
at Rockefeller Center in New York - April 8, 2002.

I was named International Franchise Association
Entrepreneur of the Year in 2006.

Opening a Liberty Tax store in my hometown of Buffalo, NY.

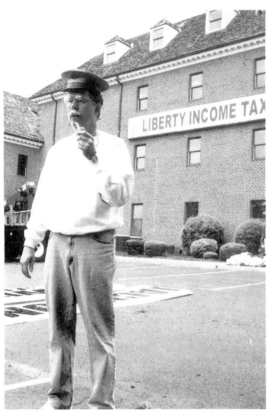

As we replaced the Jackson Hewitt sign with Liberty Tax at our first headquarters building, I played the role of General Douglas MacArthur – I have returned!

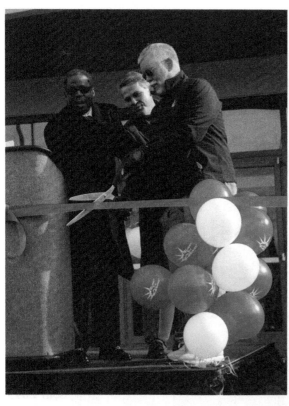

Grand Opening of Building #2 on the current Liberty Tax campus in Virginia Beach in 2010.

We went public in 2012 (NASDAQ: TAX) Martha, Gordon and I at the NASDAQ podium.

Set unrealistic goals. You never know where this will take you. July, 2012.

Interacting with franchisees during our 2013 Convention and cocktail party.

To think that Sandy Raiter was afraid of computers? She became one of our best employees and tax/technology wiz.

At our yearly convention, I spend hours answering questions directly from our franchisees.

Mom joins me at our
2014 Convention.

A Liberty Tax
victory - We Compete!

Chapter 8
Give Loyalty, Get Loyalty

When we began this story, I mentioned that throughout my life people have said I'm unique. I agree and take this as a compliment. My nature is different in several ways: staying in the zone of bliss, my love of reading as a young child, and my commitment to loyalty. Let's revisit bliss. Remember when you were young; you think you can do anything. Then it feels like everyone beats you down: your teachers, your friends, your enemies saying, "You can't do this or that." Even though naysayers, both internal and external, bludgeoned me, they never beat me down. People still try to stop me all the time, but I never go to sleep or wake up saying, "Oh, the end is near; there is no way I can maneuver through this." I have tons of stress and many barriers to overcome. Even through the previous year's excruciating trials and challenges – 1995 was the worst of the worst – I never left this zone of bliss. I don't live with doubt; I have always had this underlying feeling that I'm going to be successful.

Give Back and Set an Example

Next, as a kid, I became a voracious reader. By the time I entered third grade, I was reading books like *The Last of the Mohicans*. As a teenager, I devoured huge, great novels like *Gone with the Wind* and *War and Peace*. I like books and movies with happy endings, where the good guy wins and the honorable team is victorious.

I was frequently reading books about heroes – whether it was Superman or some other note-worthy character of virtue – and I always envisioned myself playing that part. I guess you could say I bought into the hero thing - that you have to do the right thing. You have to give back and set an example.

While being a hero isn't overtly in my mind, somewhere in the back of my consciousness I have to strive to be the best and almost bigger than life. This has manifested itself in many ways. As I got older, whenever I went out to dinner or lunch with anyone I would try to pay, even though sometimes I couldn't afford it. I felt that I had to do more for every person than they did for me. This fanatical commitment wasn't a conscious thing. I didn't realize that I had this extreme need to give until a few years ago. This way of thinking is just part of my DNA.

Unconditional Loyalty

This leads to another way I'm different: the loyalty factor. I'm loyal to a fault. It's both a strength and one of my major weaknesses. This really started with my father who set many examples of loyalty. When I was young, my parents lived on a small budget and Mom struggled to feed us. Money was a contentious issue in our family. My parents eventually became multi-millionaires, but growing up we barely had enough to live on. Dad would save money for safety – he would sock money away. Both of his parents died when he was a teenager, his mother when he was about 13 and his father when he was 19, so he really didn't have any backup. He grew up during the Depression and his family was incredibly poor, so he lived that kind of mentality.

It was very difficult on my mom and most members of her family shunned him. Granted, Dad was a solitary person. My mom's older sister divorced and was living hand to mouth, raising four children. There wasn't any significant welfare back in the 1950s, so even though Mom's family disregarded him, every month my dad would write a check and mail it to them. Even though our family barely had enough, this very private, introverted man who was misunderstood by others, always found a way to give. So I learned loyalty from my dad and the way he cared not only for friends, but people who didn't even like him. He went way over and above what most people do. This is just one of many examples of loyalty I learned from my dad.

Be The Voice Of Optimism

I mentioned my reluctance to let people go in my business. I give people too many chances. It's an error I've made because I go too far in letting people stay around too long. I guess from a holistic, life approach it sort of feels better. On the other hand, I've had to learn it's best to let people go find somewhere else to be extraordinary quicker. That is the better course of action because there is another factor in the loyalty equation: loyalty to yourself. To thine own self be true. This was part of the lesson and the choice I had to make in 1996.

Another lesson I learned during this season is when you give loyalty, you get loyalty in return. This has become a guiding principle in building Liberty Tax today and one of the key reasons we thrive. For Jackson Hewitt then, loyalty to my franchisees and employees was the main reason I stuck it out for as long as I did. After our previous year, the franchisees were demoralized and fear pervaded our entire industry. There were still many unknowns about external factors like the IRS, and there was also fear internally. I had to put on a bold face and adopt the attitude that we were going to turn this around. It

was important that I continued that positive message during this struggle. It was my job to stand in front of the troops and never waiver in my belief or my voice of optimism. We had an incredible year as a result of this.

The Tree that Bends Bounces Back

In 1996, the IRS also reacted well and came back strong. Sometimes in a storm, the tree that bends bounces back the other way. The IRS was extremely easy to work with after being spanked by Congress. Even the irate customers came back and when that happened – to our benefit – we would get the monies from the previous year, if they were past due. It was a robust year with an incredible increase in profit. With the bank loan in place and our board seats full, we opened the season with 1,342 offices. Jackson Hewitt's sales were up 48%. Profits more than tripled, as earnings per share jumped from 11 cents the year before to 40 cents.

These excellent results enabled us to purchase back almost all of the warrants we issued to NationsBank the previous fall. We reclaimed the 10% ownership we forfeited to secure the loan. Jackson Hewitt recovered. Now the question remained, how would the board structure our leadership? On July 1, 1996 the fifth person on the board, Keith Alessi, became president and CEO of Jackson Hewitt and I continued on as chairman of the board. Keith lived more than three hours away, in the mountains, and would drive in every Monday and drive home Thursday night. This was a very different leadership approach for our company. Keith was a great public speaker and salesman. I was a business operator.

A Business Divided Cannot Stand

Without getting into the minutiae of our differences, suffice it to say the franchisees and employees were caught in the middle. You can only imagine how loyalty became a divisive issue and many employees found it difficult to survive. Employees who were loyal to me, or even perceived to be loyal to me, suffered and I was powerless to stop it. The culture shift I had felt in 1995 became a full-blown clash of cultures between old and new. A business divided cannot stand, even as the stock price was rising.

The new culture brought a different concern for the franchisees. They had to expand or they would lose their territories. This meant franchisees had to grow quickly, opening territories they had not yet developed. My many years in the business had taught me the hard lesson of managing growth because the alternative could be bankruptcy.

Know When to Walk Away

In September 1996, I made a decision based on loyalty. For my trusted employees, I couldn't put them in the middle of a clash of cultures anymore. For our franchisees, I wouldn't go along with the new style of management. For me – to thine own self be true – I felt the pull of liberty elsewhere. I left Jackson Hewitt, the company that still bears my name. I cleaned out my desk and walked away from the business I built and operated for almost 15 years, 50,000 stock options (which would eventually be worth $3.2 million), and an annual salary of $250,000. At that point, I still owned 5% of the company. What I didn't realize, at the time, was that my loyal friends would stay with me. Give loyalty, get loyalty.

Once I left, people close to me became casualties of the transition. Sue Ventresca, one of the original Jackson Hewitt investors, a corporate manager and franchise owner, was asked to leave the board of directors. She sold her franchises back to the company and retired. Keith told Jack Seal, Director of Field Operations, that his only option was to run company stores as a district manager—a position far below his current one. Jack negotiated the purchase of franchises in Las Vegas and a severance package. Prior to Keith forcing his hand, he didn't intend to leave the company or his position.

For Martha O'Gorman, the choice was very difficult. She had been with the company for 10 years. I talked with her a couple of weeks before I left and she said, "I don't know if I can leave here because this is my identity. Who am I if I'm not the Director of Communications for Jackson Hewitt?" I always want what's best for every person I'm dealing with. I told her, "If it's best for you to leave, that's great, but if not, you need to stay." She left Jackson Hewitt within a month and would go on to become one of the founders of Liberty. At that same time, Donna Halligan, corporate manager and franchisee, turned in her resignation.

Go More than the Extra Mile

After Labor Day I never set foot in Jackson Hewitt headquarters again, but as Chairman of the Board I still did everything I could to encourage the employees and put out proverbial fires for the franchisees. In one case, it meant rolling up my sleeves and schlepping boxes. Franchisee, Jeff Dusza, ran three locations in a Houston mall when the walls came crashing down. Literally. On a Saturday morning in January 1997 – the middle of our peak season – a construction crew was building an attachment to the mall. The crew hit the main support beam with a wrecking ball and a huge section of the mall col-

lapsed. The disaster killed three women. When it became clear that the Jackson Hewitt corporate office had other priorities, Martha and I immediately got on a plane and headed to the crumpled Northline Mall in Houston.

Jeff remembers, "I called Keith, the CEO of Jackson Hewitt, and didn't get any help. I reached out to John and he said 'I'll be on the next flight out.' When he arrived, he started giving orders like he always does. He told me to go rent computers. He sent Martha to negotiate for another, bigger space. We had boxes of customers' checks and cash amid the rubble, and John helped schlep all the boxes out of there. We had a short amount of time to get in and get out because this had turned into a crime scene and if it weren't for John, we wouldn't have had a chance. He set us up in a warehouse and that helped mitigate our losses. We recovered because of what he did."

Secretly, I was praying for my life the whole time. The mall was closed down, and I was afraid what was left of the building would collapse on us. This was not normal work for a chairman of the board and founder of a public company.

I focused on doing anything and everything I could to help the franchisees including running marketing for Jack Seal in Las Vegas. I spent my own money to fly out there and help train his people on whatever they needed, from customer service to policies and procedures. In the meantime, Martha and I had been talking about building a new tax business with guiding principles, rooted in integrity.

When You Give to Others, Life Gives Back

I've found that when you give to others, life gives back to you. During that Las Vegas trip, a fortunate thing happened. I drove by the Liberty Square strip mall on West Sahara Avenue, where there was a 25' tall Statue of Liberty. It gave me an idea. We had been looking for something tangible, an icon with both meaning and marketing potential. Most people, within 10-15 minutes of the Statue of Liberty, would remember that she is there. Liberty could be a logo that is a tangible object, not just an idea. That's a huge competitive advantage for branding. In the future, when someone was driving by our offices that's how they would see us from 50-100 yards away. What could be better than Liberty Tax Service? I called our attorney, Kathleen Curry, right away to see if we could get the trademark. Sure enough, no one had thought of this and we secured this great name. Here I had made myself available to any Jackson Hewitt franchisee that wanted and appreciated help, and I was the one who ended up receiving this gift of Liberty.

To Get Loyalty, You Must First Give Loyalty

You don't get loyalty without giving it first. Just because you are the boss doesn't mean that you automatically get loyalty. You have to give it and show it and prove it. During this time, I felt the pain of the people who turned on me or didn't believe in me. In truth, that's just as motivating for me as the people who stick with me. I want to show them I can win. It's harder for me to write about – even speak about – the people who have been my loyal friends over the years. Those feelings go deeper than words. The dream of liberty and the gift of loyalty were about to take us on a new journey: building the fastest growing tax franchise company in this country, growing the right way.

I suppose there is one last lesson in giving loyalty. God, the universe, the laws of nature and business came into play in a huge way. Fast forward to October 31, 1998. Jackson Hewitt sold 305 franchise territories, compared to 85 the previous year and budgeted to open 1900 stores in January 1998. The stock price kept rebounding. It traded the previous summer at $8 per share, climbed to $17, and shares sold as part of a public offering were $22.50. Jackson Hewitt raised approximately $23 million.

> "Because of the public offering, Keith got to go to Wall Street and tell the story–a great story–and while he's telling the story, the stock was just climbing. The reviewer from the SEC said 'What's happening?' I said, 'nothing new'. Really, it was nothing new, people were just learning the story–learning what a great company it was. Keith was now selling this business that John built. It was a great combination. Then later the stock got to something like $54 per share and Keith called me. He had gotten a call from HFS. I asked who they were. He said, 'They are a big franchisor, they own Ramada and other hotels.' I said, 'What do they want?' Keith said, 'To buy Jackson Hewitt.'"
> **- John Paris, *Former Counsel to Jackson Hewitt***

When the deal was completed, HFS made a tender offer for all outstanding Jackson Hewitt shares and stock options at $68 per share. HFS, which would soon merge with Cendant Corporation, paid $483 million dollars for Jackson Hewitt. The bottom line is if you had invested $5000 in August 1982, that investment would have grown to $2,000,000 by December 1997.

Checkmate! Liberty, here we come.

JOHN'S PRINCIPLES TO LIVE BY

- Give back and set an example
- Show unconditional loyalty
- Be the voice of optimism
- The tree that bends bounces back
- A business divided cannot stand
- Know when to walk away
- Go more than the extra mile
- When you give to others, life gives back
- To get loyalty, you must first give loyalty

Your Challenge

How can you give loyalty in your business, above and beyond anything that is normal or expected?

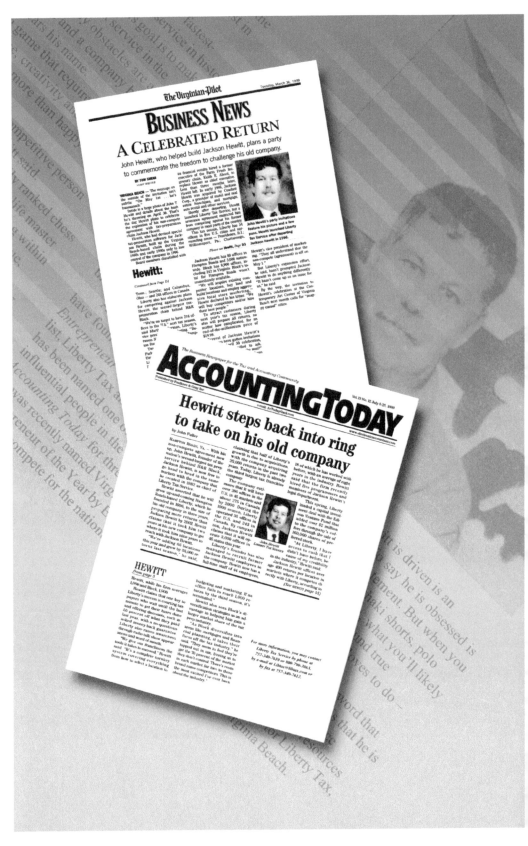

Chapter 9
Create Raving Fans

It all started on a napkin. Or maybe I should say, our vision continued and was refined on a napkin. Hold this napkin thought for a moment – I'll get to it. The bad news was we were starting again. The good news was we were starting again.

I spent much of my time deciding what to do next. I felt capable of running any business in any industry. As I contemplated my next step, I realized the competitive environment in the tax industry was just too good to pass up. The same opportunities that made it a great business before made it a great opportunity now. I knew the tax preparation business better than anyone else and with the rise of the World Wide Web, a new way to compete - iCompete - would add a new dimension to dominate business using the Internet. Plus, there was room for a third brand with a strategic vision. With all the mistakes I'd made and lessons learned, I knew I would do a better job the second time around. If you build a business for 15 years and get a chance to start all over again, you better be able to do it a lot better or you're an idiot.

If you have ever had to start all over again, you'll understand. Fortunately, I'm in good company. Steve Jobs was fired from his own company, and Abraham Lincoln failed in business, had a nervous breakdown, and was defeated in eight elections.[6] Before Walt Disney experienced massive success, he filed for bankruptcy once and skated on the edge of disaster later in his career.[7] Thomas Edison viewed challenges as a learning experience. As one of America's most well-known and prolific innovators, Edison became famous for saying, "I have not failed 10,000 times. I have not failed once. I have succeeded in proving that those 10,000 ways will not work. When I have eliminated the ways that will not work, I will find the ways that will work."[8] There are just zillions of failures before you get to massive success. You cannot achieve massive success without massive failure. Mistakes, challenges, and failures are simply a wise person's education.

Set Unrealistic Goals

After Martha and Jack left Jackson Hewitt, we began planning for a bigger and better company. After attending an IRS show in San Diego, we all sat at a restaurant and started talking about how we would do things differently the

second time around. We wanted to have fun! We wanted to create an environment of success and we began planning how we would become the largest tax service in the universe by 2020. A lot of tequila fueled our creative thinking and together, we wrote on the back of a napkin ten things we would do better to create an environment of success: our "Ten Commandments."

The folklore of the napkin is well known at Liberty today. At one time, we even distributed napkin idea notebooks for inspiration. We kept some of the ideas and they became the foundation for our core principles. We threw out other ideas in the spirit of improving every day and monitoring results. Here are the Ten Commandments on our napkin (with my additional commentary):

1) **Keep control of company stock** – This is a lesson Steve Jobs also learned the hard way in losing control of Apple. At Jackson Hewitt, I didn't have controlling stock and we agreed that we didn't ever want that to happen again. Entrepreneurs need to be careful because I mistakenly believed that as long as I was doing a great job, I would have control of the company. People and events beyond anyone's control can get in the way of that. From now on, I would keep controlling interest in my company. One word of caution here – in many entrepreneurial ventures, the company outgrows the capability of the entrepreneur. That's normal in normal business. So this advice isn't for everyone. Most people can only grow a business so far and then they need professional management. Many leaders are incapable of improving and managing growth from one office to 1,000 offices to 10,000 offices, so a leadership change may be necessary. There is a time to let go of a smaller vision to reach a larger goal.

2) **Get rid of people with bad attitudes more quickly.** This is still one of my weaknesses. People with bad attitudes are toxic on the people around them for a lot of reasons. When you walk down the hall and see this person, you just feel worse. Other employees also feel underappreciated if Mr. or Mrs. Negativity is given additional compensation. Let's say someone went around and yelled and screamed for ten seconds. So why can't someone else yell and scream for ten seconds? You're creating a lower standard of culture and happiness. You're also allowing a higher standard

of tolerance for bad behavior if you keep these people around. It looks like you are rubber-stamping their culture-breaking behaviors without actually saying so. The secret to having a great culture is first hiring people with great attitudes. Then, knowing you're going to be wrong sometimes, you have to manage out the people who don't fit the culture. This is very hard because I don't want to see anyone get hurt or go without a job, so it's been a very difficult commandment for me to enforce.

Several years ago, I had a meeting in my office at Liberty Tax that was a learning experience for me. We had a guy who worked in technology who had attended our prior management retreat. He argued with me, in a very pessimistic way, in front of 50 people. Don't get me wrong, I appreciate it when someone speaks his or her mind, but this guy brought down the whole team. I said to our head of technology, Charlie Kirkpatrick, I really don't think this employee should come to the next management retreat because he's too negative. Charlie felt he should be at this meeting, so I said I would only consider it if he comes and meets with me personally.

During the meeting, I asked this guy, "Are you an optimist or a pessimist?" He said, "I don't think I'm either. I like to feel that I'm a realist." He didn't believe he fit into either of those categories. He was above that. He was the first human being who ever gave me that answer; most people freely admit what they are. Realist implies being jaded, sad, and disappointed with life. That sounds like a pessimist to me.

I replied, "Think about the inanity in 1997 when I sat down with my top four people and had zero offices and I said we're not only going to beat the 800 pound gorilla, H&R Block, but we're going to grow faster than any other tax service. By 2020, we're going to be bigger than anyone, including my own name, my own system: Jackson Hewitt. Is that the real world? Is that rational? Isn't that inane and crazy? What human being would say that's likely to happen? That's unrealistic." I told him that if he's not unrealistic and willing to set high goals, then he's never going to achieve anything. He would continue to be ordinary. Attitude is everything.

In my career, I have helped almost 800 people become millionaires. This "realist" was not one of them. These are my winners, with the right attitude, and that number grows every day, every tax season. My philos-

ophy is if you're coming to work in the morning and you're not looking forward to it, you're going to the wrong place. Attitude is a "Matter of Choice" and is one of our guiding principles at Liberty Tax today.

You can take someone with a positive attitude and they can have a bad day, a bad week, a bad month, but they bounce back. If you take someone with a pessimistic attitude and they have a good hour, a good day, or a good month, they bounce back to their negative attitude. So in my career, I've hit my head against the wall trying to change numerous people's attitudes. I was never successful in doing so. The number one principle we hire for at Liberty Tax today is attitude.

3) **Only go into cities where we can achieve critical mass the first year**, where we can develop effective branding more quickly. At Jackson Hewitt, we had gone into a lot of areas and just languished. We hadn't grown to an adequate size to afford the proper marketing. For example, to go into a city like Rochester, New York we decided we would need a minimum of five offices. In growing our business, we wanted to hold off until we were ready to expand to this level. We eventually discarded this rule. These were the initial ideas that we had and as we got further into it, we learned what would work and what wouldn't as we worked to improve each day.

4) **Minimum requirement for franchisees.** This was an objective measure to assess whether or not a franchisee was doing a minimum level of customer service that was satisfactory. At the time, H&R Block was processing about 1,800 returns per office. So we set a minimum requirement of 1,000 returns by a franchisee's fourth year. We knew if they couldn't reach that number it was most likely because they were offering poor customer service. We would have the right to take back the office in order to protect the Liberty Tax brand. Whoever offered the worst customer service in the country could bring down our entire company's reputation to that level. If our goal was to be the best in the universe, setting high standards was crucial.

5) **We will always be first or second largest in the number of returns per office in the U.S.** The purpose of this principle is so we're not expanding

unprofitable locations. There are only three major firms. We would need to average in the top two in number of returns per office to assure profitability. Anything less than that and we might be expanding too rapidly, causing the growth to be too diluted. That's why it's important to be number one or two in each office, so that our franchisees would have a solid foundation for growth.

6) **Don't open new offices until over 90% of existing offices are successful.** This stemmed from the lesson of growing too quickly with Montgomery Ward in our early days, as well as the tax season of 1995. Overexpansion can kill your business and we were determined to learn from these mistakes. This principle helped ensure our franchisees have a good foundation of cash flow, so we didn't overstep and go too far. Don't try to run so fast that you fall down – expand from strength.

7) **Free franchises.** I can tell you no word has created more angst (among naysayers) and opportunity (among believers) than the word "FREE." Who gives away free franchises? Only someone with unrealistic and fanatical goals. We wanted to start out very aggressively. At that time, Jackson Hewitt was charging $25,000 per territory and in order to get some traction, initially we offered franchises with no fee the first year. You can bet this created some buzz, and this strategy served as an expansion opportunity for our initial launch. In fact, people are still talking about it. At a recent sales seminar, one man told us that he heard about Liberty Tax during the time when there was no franchise fee. Today, he was ready to pay $40,000 for something he could have had for free then.

8) **Use free coupons much more extensively.** There's that word again. At Jackson Hewitt, we would do one customer appreciation day in March. Each office would do about two to four free returns. For our new business, we expanded that immediately to 100 free returns because it was such an effective tool. FREE return marketing has become one of my top 10 principles for success today, but there are still many franchisees who don't buy into it. They will learn… eventually. We are not the first to do something for free. Some grocery stores still give out free samples of stuff. We're not the first to invent that; sampling is one of the

original forms of advertising. It works successfully in many venues for many products and services. There are multiple advantages in giving free returns including the advantage of giving back. Think about it. Giving free returns will help you gain goodwill and additional customers for the future, plus it's giving back. To whom much is given, much is required.

9) **Purchase existing businesses.** If you're my age, you may remember the old family-owned pharmacy. This was the "mom and pop" corner store passed down from generation to generation. Times have changed along with the names of those stores. Now they're known as Walgreens, CVS, Rite Aid and other large companies that have grown their brands through acquisitions and consolidations. In our industry, there were more than 70,000 of these mom and pop offices competing with about 9,000 H&R Block offices during that time. Purchasing existing businesses is a faster, more cost effective way to acquire customers. It's a tool to fuel growth that we underutilized at Jackson Hewitt. Plus, these days it's not as common for family businesses to be passed down to children. That means business owners need an exit strategy. They are going to sell someday - either sell or die. We knew we could become their exit strategy. This is another effective way to expand, a win for us and a win for the storeowners.

10) **Keep a satisfactory cash reserve.** We skated on very thin ice at Jackson Hewitt and that was one of our weaknesses. You can get by on just enough money if there are no emergencies, but stuff happens. When it does, you need cash. This was a critical lesson for us. We almost went bankrupt two different times as a result of not having a war chest with enough cash reserves. Murphy's Law - anything that can go wrong will go wrong at the worst possible time - should be taught in Business 101.

Winners See Opportunities Where Others Only See Challenges

My non-compete clause with Jackson Hewitt, covering most of the United States, caused us to turn toward Canada. I was very familiar with Canadian laws because I grew up in Buffalo, New York - a stone's throw from the border. While I was working as a tax preparer at H&R Block, I did many Canadian

tax returns. The vast majority of the Canadian population lives within 90 miles of the U.S. border, not just because it's warmer being further south, but also because many people work in the U.S. I had customers who commuted to America every week and they had to file U.S. tax returns. Plus, Canada has a very similar tax system to the U.S. and adapting to the subtle differences wouldn't present much of a problem.

In our research, we found Tax Depot, Inc., a franchised company of tax preparation offices in Canada. The company had gone bankrupt several years earlier and was just limping along with no growth. In January 1997, Jack and I first met with Gary and Steve Ibbotson, owners of Tax Depot. We found out that Tax Depot was not a true franchise, just a loose collection of tax offices using the same name without a consistent operating system. The Ibbotsons had purchased Tax Depot as a sideline to their highly successful company, Farm Business Consultants. Tax Depot had potential; it just hadn't had much attention. Jack, Donna, Martha, and I hoped to bring a wealth of experience to this table. For the next five months, we collaborated on the terms of our involvement with Tax Depot. We had a loosely formed business plan typed on a home computer in Donna's house; she was the only one of us who even had a computer.

When we acquired Tax Depot, another loyal friend, attorney Kathleen Curry left Jackson Hewitt and joined our newly formed team. I incorporated JTH Tax and bought majority ownership of Tax Depot on June 1, 1997. Remember Napkin Commandment #1: keep control of company stock. I went on to improve the ownership structure of JTH Tax, Inc. As the only Class B shareholder, I own the controlling shares of the company. No investor or group of investors can acquire enough stock, or votes on the board, to sell the company without my permission.

On September 1, 1997 JTH Tax took over the management of Tax Depot, Inc. in Canada. We were back in business! Our team brought their expertise to operations, marketing, legal and training. We began the process of updating and enhancing the Canadian operations to help the existing offices perform better. I hired Jeff Dusza, a former Jackson Hewitt franchisee and sales person, to market the business and recruit potential franchisees. We had plenty of work to be done in Canada; in the previous two years Tax Depot had shown virtually no growth.

We inherited some great employees from Tax Depot. While Canada had considerable potential, we knew there was still unlimited opportunity for JTH Tax south of the border. I picked out the major metropolitan areas in the

United States that Jackson Hewitt was not in when I left and had not opened in the 1997 season, including Columbus, Ohio, Seattle, Washington and the Tri-Cities area of Tennessee (Kingsport, Bristol, and Johnson City). We targeted those markets for expansion. Due to my non-compete, I couldn't advertise nationally to prospective franchisees. Remember Napkin Commandment #9, the best way to start a presence in these markets was to convert existing independent tax offices. Jack spearheaded the campaigns to buy our first U.S. offices.

JTH Tax sought out owners who were willing to sell their businesses or convert to franchises. Jack first negotiated the purchase of Devore Tax Service, located in downtown Columbus, Ohio. We planned to use the existing office and open several stores around it so the company would have a presence in the market.

"John called into our operating committee meeting from Canada. It was time to close on Columbus and commit to opening stores or to postpone the deal. He called for a vote and we were divided. Everyone had just been through so much turmoil and change. Canada was so small and manageable, but this would be a whole new thing. We had no software, no store managers; no tax schools had been run... it just seemed impossible. John said, 'This is good for the company; we need to get out there now and get started. I know that we can do this, but I also know that I can't do it without your support. Are you with me?' Everyone agreed. We knew John was right, he had the big picture." – *Martha O'Gorman, CMO of Liberty Tax, former Communications Director at Jackson Hewitt*

Unrealistic goals and loyal friends are a winning combination. We opened five stores in Columbus in January 1998. By the end of the season, our five Columbus stores had done 5,000 tax returns compared to Jackson Hewitt's 3,500 returns from 13 offices in that region. JTH Tax had arrived in the United States.

Understanding the Value of "FREE"

In Columbus, we also used our offices to execute a bold marketing test using Napkin Commandment #8. We prepared returns free of charge after the peak of tax season. During March, a typically slow time during the season, the tax offices needed to be open and staffed anyway. We had the capacity to do the business, just not the customers. Free returns changed all of that.

At Jackson Hewitt, we had sold a territory to a former H&R Block district manager in Terre Haute, Indiana. Block sued our franchisee for violations of his non-compete agreement and he agreed not to open that year. Losing this experienced franchisee was out of the question, so I hired him to work in operations outside of his non-compete area. He bought the franchise and ran it as a company store until his agreement expired.

In order to teach Block a lesson, that location did every return *for free* the entire tax season. We also advertised that any previous Block customer who came into the office would be paid $10 for trying our service. The first year the office prepared 1200 returns — a huge amount for a company-run, first-year office in a new market. In subsequent years, the store performed well and turned those free customers into paying ones who returned each year. Free returns worked and still work in my business today. For the small cost of doing the returns we gained repeat customers, referrals, and media exposure. The program allowed us to build the market faster.

We were off to a good start and it was time for JTH Tax to consolidate our operations in the U.S. and Canada under one name. Canada operated under their old name, U&R Tax Depot and the U.S. operated under the name of our acquisition in Columbus, DeVore Tax Service. Both of those names held no connection to our new company and to build a brand, we needed a catchy name.

Two years had passed since I had driven by the shopping center in Las Vegas with the huge Statue of Liberty. Martha remembers, "At first, the Canadian managers didn't like the name, so we didn't adopt it. However, there are distinct advantages to operating under the same name in both countries, so we kept trying. No one could come up with a name that wowed us. Finally, the Canadian managers agreed that Liberty worked for both companies. Once we developed the logo, had it printed, and I saw it on paper, that's when I knew the company would be successful. We would be bigger and better than Jackson Hewitt."

That summer, Liberty Tax Service was born. Along with our new name, we adopted a new mission statement: Set the Standard, Improve Each Day and Have Some Fun. We were determined to be more innovative, provide better service, and market at the grass roots level better than our competitors. We focused on selling franchises in Canada and the U.S. markets that weren't covered by my non-compete agreement. In tax season 1999, in addition to 214 Canadian offices, we opened 35 offices in seven U.S. markets.

In those first two years, we learned from our mistakes and established a firm base from which Liberty Tax Service would grow. On May 1, 1999, I threw a huge party, inviting all my business contacts, investors, current and former employees, and Liberty franchisees to attend. My non-compete agreement in the United States expired the day before and *Entrepreneur* magazine had just ranked the Liberty Tax Service franchise opportunity at #144 on their list of 'Top 500' franchise opportunities. Just one year before, only six months after we acquired Tax Depot, we were ranked #405. The party celebrated our freedom to grow what we had learned from our past, and most importantly, we celebrated our future. Our momentum was building.

I learned chess at a very young age and that's been an important part of my success. In business, if they make one move, we make another. If you are a master chess player, you can see many moves ahead and that's how I think about business. I'm always looking ahead and this game was about to get even more fun!

JOHN'S 10 NAPKIN COMMANDMENTS

- Keep control of company stock
- Get rid of people with bad attitudes more quickly
- Only go into cities where we can achieve critical mass the first year
- Set minimum requirements for franchisees
- We will always be the first or second largest in number of returns per office
- Don't open new offices until over 90% of existing offices are successful
- Free franchises
- Purchase existing businesses
- Use free coupons much more extensively
- Keep a satisfactory cash reserve

What are Your Napkin Commandments?

For your business, it's important to understand your marketing and branding needs before you open any office. How and where can you achieve maximum impact so you don't languish? Beyond setting minimum standards of production, how will you strive to be number one? How will you manage growth for optimum success?

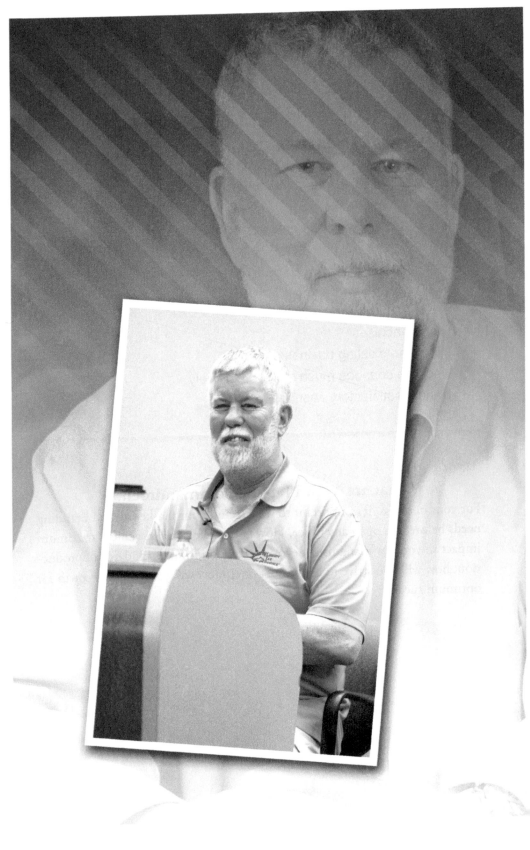

Chapter 10
Enjoy the Journey, Do it with Pride

I once heard the story of a little girl with an innocent question. It was Easter and she was watching her mom cut a ham in half in order to cook the pieces in two separate pans. She asked, "Mom, why do you cut the hambone in half?" Her mom replied, "Because that's what Grandma always did. Go ask her." So the little girl went to her grandma and asked, "Why do you always cut the hambone in half and cook the pieces in two separate pans?" Her grandmother replied, "Because that's what Great Grandma always did. Go ask her." Determined to get an answer, the little girl asked her great grandmother, "Why do you always cut the hambone in half and cook the pieces in two separate pans?" Her great grandmother replied, "Because back in the old days, we didn't have an oven big enough to fit the whole ham." So for generations they had been cutting the ham in two pieces and cooking it in two separate pans for no reason. The excuse is just as ridiculous when someone says, "This is the way we've always done it, so we can't change."

In 1899, the U.S. Commissioner of Patents, Charles H. Duell, allegedly recommended that the Patent Office be closed when he stated, "Everything that can be invented has been invented."[9] While the veracity of this quote is disputed in academic circles, unfortunately, lack of vision is very true and very destructive in business circles. Many CEOs resist change, so the corporate vision is blurred and growth is stunted. Most people accept things the way they are just because it's the way they've always been.

Create Raving Fans!

It was time for a change. Was it possible that visiting a tax preparation office could be fun? "Fun" isn't usually a word associated with taxes. What if we took a different approach? What if our customers were greeted not only by smiling, friendly tax preparers, but also by Lady Liberty or Uncle Sam? Enter the wavers! If you have ever driven by a Liberty Tax location, you may have seen our smiling, dancing marketing representatives waving at you. This idea was based on "Guerrilla Marketing," the books and teachings of the late Jay Conrad Levinson touting unique, unconventional, even disruptive approach-

es to marketing. For us, that meant fun and friendly. We created Lady Liberty and Uncle Sam costumes and encouraged franchisees to have employees dress up, wave at cars in front of their offices, and pass out coupons at local events.

Guerrilla marketing is just smart business. Our research indicated that people are twice as likely to accept a coupon from a costumed marketer, than they are from one who is dressed in normal attire. At first, many franchisees balked at this idea. We trained them, showed them the results, but they didn't believe in it or understand the importance of this type of marketing. I had to make another tough decision. During training, I decided to require every prospective franchisee or employee to put on a waver costume to see that it works. I made this decision knowing that some of the candidates would drop out. Can you be too boring to be an entrepreneur? You can! They left. Others with a sense of humor and adventure would put on the costume and wave at people. Over the years, I asked hundreds of people, "When you had the costume on, did you notice people treated you differently?" Unanimously, people said, "Yes!" People honked, smiled and waved back. This is especially true for franchisees that visited another business. Without a costume, they are often shooed out with a stern warning – no solicitation. But our wavers are rarely asked to leave because people are interested to know what's going on. A costumed character attracts positive attention. Across the country, many local newspapers and television stations have featured our wavers.

We still have naysayers who criticize our wavers. I understand that one of our competitors pelted a costumed Lady Liberty and Uncle Sam with nerf balls at their annual convention. I take this as a compliment. Others have said that no one should have to stand on a street corner and wave in costume. Let me give you a different take on our wavers – a glimpse of changed lives, with full stories recorded in our culture book, "Fanatical at Liberty."

Fanatical Wavers!

"It was two years ago and I was out of a job. I looked each day. I was getting tired, and I cried each day. I asked God to direct me to a job. I saw someone waving and I thought to myself, why not? So I went and applied.... I love people and I love to smile and try to make someone's day. I have been able to put food on the table for my family because of Liberty Tax. They gave me a reason to get out of bed in the mornings."
- Patricia Cutrell/Waver - Valdosta, GA

"For the first time, I'd felt true pride and accomplishment, in myself. I took this confidence on to other jobs, and back around to the Liberty Tax office in Everett. I'm writing all this before I start my shift at 1pm, and I've gained even more skills from working here, as well. I feel it when people honk at me, or give me a thumbs up that - for once - I'm actually good at something. Even though it's temporary, this job is the highlight of my year, and is a strong contribution on having almost four years clean from drugs."
- Michael Chenoweth/Waver- Everett, WA

"I love working at Liberty Tax and I'm a 4th year waver. In 2011, I was unemployed and was looking for a job, so I went to Liberty Tax in Waukegan, IL. I filled out an application and I did a tryout, and got the job just like that. I was so happy and excited to have something after being unemployed for a while... I love waving to people and putting smiles on their faces. People even come up to me to take a picture with them, and it just makes me feel good." **- Rebecca Raisman/Waver - Waukegan, IL**

"Liberty has helped me gain a sense of pride, a steady employment history, employment skills and a great and positive support system. Liberty Tax has truly touched and changed my life for the better."
- Timmithy Longoria/Waver and Marketing - Grande Prairie, TX

"I thank God for blessing me with this job, and I will never forget how they helped me out and made me feel like a brand new person."
– Eric Wynder/Waver – Hampton, VA

THE WALL STREET JOURNAL.

© 2006 Dow Jones & Company. All Rights Reserved

WSJ.com

MONDAY, APRIL 17, 2006 · VOL. CCXLVII NO. 80 · ★★ $1.00

Upstart Tax Preparer Surges to No. 3 Spot
Riding 'the Wavers'

Dancing Uncle Sams Lure Customers to Liberty; Dodging a Tossed Hot Dog

By **KEVIN HELLIKER**
April 17, 2006; Page A1

KANSAS CITY, Kan. — Kebba Njie was earning $6 an hour moving furniture and cleaning up messes when the opportunity arose to play Uncle Sam.

Never mind that Mr. Njie, a West African immigrant, isn't old, bearded or an American citizen. To passersby on State Avenue here, he became the

Waver Jerron Dennis and Lady Liberty outside Liberty Tax Service in Chicago.

nation's symbol.

On street corners across America, Uncle Sam waves, dances, shouts, sings and plays air guitar on behalf of a tax-preparation service. A regular companion is Lady Liberty. Her antics are similarly attention-getting. Children know that the two are often good for free Statue of Liberty crowns.

Uncle Sam and Lady Liberty have been at it since January, and today their numbers could reach a new high. As the midnight deadline approaches for filing tax returns in most states, the population of Uncle Sams and Lady Libertys on the streets of America could hit 3,000.

Tomorrow, all will be gone.

"Uncle Sam gets hung up for another year," says Willis Tyus, the most popular of several Uncle Sams on 39th Street here in Kansas City, Kan.

Uncle Sam and Lady Liberty are the creations of a tax-preparation industry pioneer named John Hewitt. After building a firm called Jackson Hewitt Inc. into the industry's second-largest player behind H&R Block Inc., Mr. Hewitt orchestrated a sale of Jackson Hewitt, resigned and soon afterward started a new company,

Liberty Tax Service. To get customers into Liberty's doors, he started hiring costumed wavers. The strategy seemed ill-advised to some because costumed wavers — for instance, the Chick-fil-A restaurant cows that hold signs saying Eat Mor Chikin — generally personify the promise of food and fun. By contrast, Uncle Sam and Lady Liberty tout the promise of a well-prepared Form 1040.

When a Florida official of H&R Block took a page out of Liberty's book by dressing up as a big green block, H&R headquarters wasn't amused.

"This was off-strategy and that person was reprimanded for doing it," says an H&R Block spokeswoman. "Americans expect an experienced, highly trained tax professional to lead them through the myriad of tax-law changes. That's why H&R Block is

We are changing lives and having some fun along the way. Fun and taxes? Whoever dreamed those words would go together? We did, and quite possibly, so did my son. It turns out Julio, the win or die-trying kid from the middle school basketball team has nothing on Danny, who has taken guerrilla market-

ing to the major leagues. "Let's talk fanatical," adds Danny. "I've traveled the world, 200 days per year, in a Liberty costume! Planes, trains, and automobiles – everywhere I went – football and basketball games. Our team even showed up at a Snoop Dog concert in Chico, California. I had six people in costumes with me carrying big bags of Dum Dums (competitors – oops, I meant candy). They loved us! One year, I flew into Chicago and brought about 2,000 Statue of Liberty crowns to celebrate the 4th of July at a Cubs game. I had 15 people helping me when I received a text from one of our franchisees, asking if we were in town. I told him yes. He replied, "I can tell, I'm at the Cubs game!" You never know where we'll show up. We never stop having fun!

We do enjoy this journey and the results speak for us. We are now the fastest growing tax franchise operation in the industry, along with a few more accolades.

> «**Top Franchises for Veterans -** *USA Today*
> *– Franchising Today*
> Liberty Tax Service has been selected for this honor from among over 200 participants, as a direct result of our commitment to the recruitment and advancement of veterans within our company. Published in June 20, 2014 issue of *USA Today – Franchising Today*
>
> «**Franchise 500 –** "**Ranked #21**"
> *– Entrepreneur Magazine,* **2014**
> Liberty Tax has consistently ranked in the Top 30 franchises of the Top 500 companies to make *Entrepreneur's* prestigious Franchise 500 list for over a decade. More than 3,000 franchises are considered each year.
>
> « **Franchise 100 -** *Franchise Gator,* **2014**
> Liberty Tax Service has made the first ever *Franchise Gator's* list of **Franchise 100.**
>
> « **The 2014 Top 50 Franchises**
> *– Franchise Business Review*
> Liberty Tax is #6 in the Finance & Tax category and #45 for its size in the 250+ class.

« Top 100 *Franchises in Canada – Be the Boss*
Liberty Tax is # 29 in the list of Top 100 Franchises in Canada.

« Top 100 *Global Franchises – Franchise Direct #19*

« Best of Readers' Choice Award
– *Coastal Virginia Magazine* **2014**
Readers from *Coastal Virginia Magazine* have recognized Liberty Tax as the overall award winner in the Best of Reader's Choice Awards for 2014 for Best Tax Service. The magazine has Liberty Tax as the 757 Gold Winner (Overall Winner), beating out local as well as other national entries.

« Best Places to Work in Virginia 2014
– "Best Company Group" – *Virginia Business*
Virginia Business honored Liberty Tax by naming it one of the Commonwealth's best employers. #31 in Large Employer Category (250 or more US employees) in 2014.

« Best Places to Work Hall of Fame
– *Inside Business* **magazine**
Since 2006, Liberty Tax has been recognized as a "Best Places to Work" company in its hometown area of Hampton Roads, Virginia.

« Best of the Best – *U.S. Veterans Magazine,* **2014**
U.S. Veterans Magazine (USVM) has credited Liberty Tax Service for their employment efforts for veterans. The results of USVM's 2014 survey were recently released after the magazine polled hundreds of Fortune 1000 companies for the evaluations. Once again, the magazine recognized Liberty Tax on the "Best of the Best" of the Nation's Top Veteran-Friendly Companies list.

« Best of the 757 – Readers' Choice Award,
Hampton Roads Magazine

« Top 100 Tax Firms – *Accounting Today* **2014**

« John Hewitt - named one of the accounting profession's Top 100 most influential people for 15 straight years
– *Accounting Today*

Improve Each Day

We also made a commitment to improve each day. That starts with me. Martha once said, "One thing that makes John different is the fact that he's committed to improving. He's always getting better. One example is his public speaking and how he went from not doing this at all, to doing a little bit, to doing a great job at it. Most people can't overcome those kinds of fears and doubts without really having the drive and the passion. I've never seen anyone go from being petrified of public speaking to now being able to speak in front of thousands of people. In 2006, when he first received Entrepreneur of the Year (by the International Franchise Organization out of 3000 franchises), he had to speak in front more than 2200 people."

Here's my version of that story. I couldn't eat anything. I sat there at the table beforehand with my family and friends around me. Well-known people, like Mary Matalin and James Carville, were sitting right up front – about 15 feet away. I didn't need any opposing viewpoints; I just wanted to get through it. I still don't like public speaking, but I am committed to improving every day.

Set the Standard

When I say, "Set the Standard," I don't mean just in this industry. We want to set a standard in which other companies around the world look up to us. First of all, we're committed to being champions of customer service. Most CEOs, over recent years, have defined their job as enhancing shareholder value. That's not my primary focus. What matters most is exceeding client expectations. If there are no customers, you don't need a Board of Directors, you don't need a CEO, and you don't need any employees or offices. I segment customer service into several categories: 1) poor, 2) average, 3) extraordinary, and fourth is fanatical- the top of the top. It's past extraordinary. Today at Liberty, I give out $1000 "Fanatical Awards" for my team members who go more than the extra mile, like Maureen Parkhill, a franchisee from Tyler, Texas.

THE BEST FREE RETURN!
Maureen Parkhill/Zee - Tyler, TX - Fanatical Award Winner!

Last week, a woman came in to do her tax returns for 2012 and 2013. She told our preparer that she still owed the IRS $711 for 2011. She had not done her 2012 return because she was afraid she would owe money and she just could not deal with it. She also told our preparer that her daughter and son-in-law had moved in with them over a year ago, and her husband was quite ill and had not worked much. All of this was putting a tremendous amount of stress on her.

Surprisingly, she and her husband were getting a $1300+ refund for 2013. She told our preparer that she could not afford to pay very much for each of these returns. She left to go to work at Dillard's across the street from our office.

Our preparer came to me to ask what we should do. I mulled the situation over and decided to do both returns for free. The 2013 refund would come very, very close to covering the 2011 and 2012 debt to the IRS if not wiping it clean. That way, the stress of owing the IRS would not continue to hang over their heads. I called her at work and told her what we were going to do. She started crying, thanked me, and said she would be in after work.

When she came in, she pulled me aside. She began thanking me again, crying, and then told me something that was gut wrenching. Their 4-month-old granddaughter had died 3 weeks before. She told me that doing these taxes for free made her feel that maybe there was hope. That perhaps this was a sign that they all would survive and life would be okay one day.

When I made that decision to do both returns for free I had two motivations. One was, of course, why we do free returns - so that we gain a paying client next year and create raving fans. My much stronger motivation was just to help someone climb out of a hole with the IRS. At the time I made the call, I had no idea what this family had been through and how much a small act of kindness could mean. I think in the seven years we have been doing this, that was the BEST free return we have ever done!

Setting the standard at Liberty also means doing things that other companies don't do, like developing a Culture Committee to help us enjoy this journey, give back, and find ways to improve everyday. The key to our success is happy, successful franchisees and happy, successful employees. If you do what you always did, you get what you always got. The corollary to that in business is if you do what all the other companies do, you produce the same results. Our goal is to create a culture of extraordinary results. If you are going to pave the way, you have to have uniqueness, not simply better execution.

Keep in Touch with All of Your Employees

I've mentioned that I meet with my employees every week to discuss these principles. We call this the "On Time" group because I shut the door exactly at 9:00 a.m. If you are not on time, you can't join us. Call it corporate tough love. I began holding this On Time group because I recognized that my training stopped with the employees who reported directly to me. My principles for success didn't even go to the next level. Anything they learned or didn't learn – it just stayed there. That meant others in the organization were not being trained and motivated. I knew it was time for another improvement.

In our meetings, I let our employees know that it's okay to make mistakes. I make it a point to challenge and annoy them in order to improve them. You have to get people out of their comfort zones. Once we debated the most important attribute in building a business. Is it communication? Excellent attitudes? Passion for your work? Several brave employees made their case for these attributes and more. I told them I believe *perseverance* is the most important attribute in building a successful business. The secret to success is to never give up. All of the principles, lessons, and character traits we've discussed mean nothing if you throw in the towel. It's do or die. If you quit, then it's over. I'm looking for leaders in my company who will persevere and set unrealistic goals. That sounds like the Goepper family and their dreams of Olympic proportions.

The Goeppers celebrate competition of Olympic proportions.

LIBERTY TAX AND THE OLYMPICS
By Linda Goepper/Zee - Lawrenceburg, IN
(Fanatical Award Winner and Olympic Mom!)

Liberty Tax and the Olympics? Our Liberty Tax business created an incredible platform for us to raise our family. We have four children, and they have all seen what it takes to build a business—risk, drive, creativity, hard work, and perseverance. They have all helped—they have participated in parades, cleaned the office, worked the festivals and helped with maintenance projects. They have seen the highs and the lows. They live with the philosophy of Set the Standard, Improve Each Day and Have Some Fun. We live this mission statement and have used this to help our kids understand how to attack life.

Nick, our oldest son, medaled in the 2014 Olympics. We have two daughters that are competitive gymnasts. Our youngest does a little bit of everything. Wow. How could this happen? Liberty Tax. We were able to create a unique schedule with our work and family to allow the kids to pursue their dreams. And, they learned how to do this, by modeling their parents and what we were able to teach them through our involvement with Liberty. They have worked with us, they have attended conventions, and they have created relationships with employees –learning about all different types of people.

Nick has handled the media in a relaxed and mature way. Kasey (age 17) coordinated a lot of the media and post-Olympic events. Bradee tackled her fear of cameras and interviews, and Jason learned to communicate with the Russians and to lead us to our destinations. They have always been part of the Liberty Tax world and they have been able to take their experiences with our business and apply it to great life adventures. Nick has worked hard. He has set goals. He has fallen down and learned to get right back up. He knows that creativity sets you apart. He knows you have to be fanatical about what you do in order to be successful. Nick's ski flew off during a competition and he just landed on one ski and kept going. Nick motivates me---and I am his mom, how crazy is that?

Liberty is a game changer. I'm always trying to change people to make them better. On a personal level, Liberty is a vehicle to do this and pay it forward in an exponential way. Whether they are franchisees, employees, area developers or stockholders, the Liberty family enables me to feel good about making a difference in the world and changing people's lives for the better. I tell my franchisees they can "ask John," when they have a question about their own businesses. I am an underutilized resource for franchisees. Many of them don't believe me when I say I'm here to help them. People don't want to bother me, but the ones who take a chance and send an email get a reply. I read quickly and I will let you know if you bother me, which almost never happens.

Enjoy the Journey, Do it With Pride

Sandy Stow, Vice President of Area Development, is one of my success stories. While Liberty has changed her life financially, her biggest concern was her daughter, Katie. No hambone inquiries from this little girl. Instead she had another set of questions. Sandy picks up the story from here, "She was 9-years-old and I didn't want to put her in daycare. So John said, 'What if we put a desk for her in your office, and we can have the bus drop her off here? Your husband can swing by later, because he gets off of work before you do. He can pick her up and go home, and when you're off, you're off.' I said "yes." Katie grew up at Liberty and had her own desk. A few times, she would go to John's office and say, 'Mr. John, my mom is busy. Can you help me with my homework?' He always did. He would also write extra addition problems for her on my office white board."

Enjoy the journey, do it with pride. On August 13, 2012 we rang the bell on Wall Street for the first time. Katie came with us dressed in a Liberty costume. At age 21, she came to visit recently and gave me the kind of hug a 9-year-old child would give. To this day, Katie still calls me "Mr. John." I believe people never fully grow up. You and I are still a certain percentage child and a certain percentage adult. It was the percentage of child that rose up in her when she came over and hugged me.

On a larger scale, to date I have created more than 800 millionaires. From the early lessons of H&R Block, to the challenges and success of Jackson Hewitt, to the industry-leading phenomenon of Liberty Tax Service, the results speak for themselves built on my 46 years of experience in the tax business, resulting in thousands of transformed lives. You would think this is a fine place to end this story. That would be normal. Not so fast - this is where the journey really takes off.

Katie joins us in celebrating at the NASDAQ podium

LIBERTY'S PRINCIPLES TO LIVE BY

- Create raving fans!
- Be honest, show respect and have integrity
- Monitor results not activities
- Mistakes are a wise person's education
- Challenge yourselves, challenge each other, break boundaries
- Give loyalty – get loyalty
- Communication, communication, communication
- Attitude is a matter of choice – you make the right choice.
- Enjoy the journey – do it with pride!
- Contribute to the team

Your Challenge

How will you set the standard, improve each day and have some fun?

Part Four: Giving Back

Thur-Sun, Dec 30, 2004-Jan 2, 2005

Rush of donations from USA is immediate and immense

Millions pledged for disaster relief

By Barbara Slavin
USA TODAY

John Hewitt is used to opening his checkbook when disaster strikes overseas.

The Virginia Beach entrepreneur, who typically gives a quarter-million dollars to charitable organizations each year, says he expects to provide as much or more to help buy food for victims of the tsunami that has killed nearly 80,000 people and devastated parts of a dozen nations that rim the Indian Ocean.

Hewitt, owner and chief executive of Liberty Tax Service, which prepared nearly 1 million tax returns last year, says he will "donate something for every tax return we do" to Stop Hunger Now, a charity in Raleigh, N.C., that is among dozens of U.S. organizations rushing aid to southern Asia and East Africa. "My feeling is that God wants us to give back," says Hewitt, 55. "I don't think God just says arbitrarily, 'You win, you lose.'"

Hewitt is among tens of thousands of Americans who are pledging support to one of the largest disaster-relief efforts in history. United Nations Secretary-General Kofi Annan says billions of dollars will be needed to feed the hungry, prevent the spread of deadly diseases and help millions of people in Asia and Africa rebuild shattered communities.

Gut-wrenching images on television of dead children, mourning survivors and inundated villages have triggered an extraordinary response among charitable organizations, faith-based groups, businesses and communities of U.S.-based immigrants from South Asia. From Northern California to New Jersey, immigrant communities are rushing to collect money, blankets, canned food and clothing. President Bush and charity groups on Wednesday urged donors to send only money because it can be used to provide aid more immediately.

As relief flights touched down Wednesday in some of the worst hit communities in Indonesia and Sri Lanka, groups across the USA were reporting a huge outpouring for victims of the tsunami, which left millions homeless and flattened communities that now need fresh water, food and medical supplies to prevent outbreaks of cholera and other diseases.

"People have lost everything," says Scott Faiia, the country director in Sri Lanka for CARE, an international anti-poverty group. "It's just a complete wipeout." Some victims have complained that aid has been slow in arriving, Faiia says, but "my personal feeling — and I've been working in relief and development for 30 years — is it was a pretty good response."

In person and on the Web

In the United States, fundraising efforts have ranged from deeply personal efforts by family members of tsunami victims to relatively anonymous donations made via Web sites operated by businesses and charities.

In Moreno Valley, Calif., east of Los Angeles, Saranasiri Wadhogala, priest at the Sambuddhaloka Buddhist temple, has collected more than $15,000 for a Sri Lanka relief fund.

Wadhogala, who is from the hard-hit Sri Lankan town of Galle, says he learned that the tsunami swept his aunt and uncle to their deaths on Sunday. Other relatives "are alive, they survive, but all their properties are damaged," he says. He plans to go to Galle soon to give the money to

In Banda Aceh, Indonesia: A father tends to his injured daughter.

charities to "build houses and to buy clothes and food."

Other donors turned to technology to send aid quickly. Catholic Relief Services reported that it had raised more than $1 million in less than three days and that it's Web site — which accepts donations by credit card — crashed because of heavy traffic. Amazon.com posted a request for donations on its home page and reported raising more than $2.5 million in 24 hours.

In Northern California, where

In Khao Lak, Thailand: Kosol Warehekul prays Wednesday for the soul of his sister, who was swept out to sea in Sunday's tsunami at the tidal goods to tourists at a beach resort. More than 1,500 people died in Thailand.

thousands of immigrants from India and other nations hit by the tsunami have flocked to work in the high-tech industry, a group called Auction Drop is urging people to drop off used digital cameras, computers and other electronic devices at UPS Stores across the country. The group will sell the items on eBay, and the proceeds will go to CARE's tsunami fund.

"The response so far has been tremendous," says Mary McClymont, president and chief executive officer of InterAction, a consortium of more than 160 U.S.-based charities. "Our members have long been aware of the generous American public. But obviously, it's a heart-wrenching tragedy, and the images on TV remind people of the devastation and grave need."

Nancy Lindborg, president of Mercy Corps, says that Portland, Ore.-based charitable organization has raised more than $1 million so far, one of the biggest collections in its 25-year history.

Besides the scope of the disaster, she attributes the response to the fact that many Americans have relatives and friends in the stricken region and that during the holidays, "people are feeling open and connected" to others.

Catholic Relief Services President Ken Hackett compares the outpouring of donations to the responses after famine in Ethiopia became widely known in 1984 and after Hurricane Mitch devastated Central

Chapter 11
The Fortunate Must Give Back

I've heard that they tell a joke about me at Jackson Hewitt. Ready for this? What's the difference between God and John Hewitt? God doesn't think he's John Hewitt. That's so true! Some people call me cocky, arrogant - even abrasive. Maybe. I call myself confident. If you have the achievements to back it up, you can also call yourself confident. In your game of life and business, will you choose to be a winner or a loser? Just normal or extraordinary? Will you choose to be a fanatical entrepreneur and how will you measure your results? Today, I measure my greatest achievements not by sales, but by giving back and changing lives. We operate a company that is famous for our culture and giving back is at the center of this.

A Deal with God

When I was struggling financially, I still wanted to tithe (donating traditionally 10% of income) but I couldn't mentally grasp it. I felt that I just didn't have enough money. So I made a deal with God. I said, "I can't afford to give 10%, but as soon as I get over this hump, I'm going to give way more than 10%." As soon as I started giving a lot of money, I received more and more. It seemed like that was an escalation point in my life and my business career. Giving became a game changer for me. This is where I formulated one of my theories: you can't give more than you receive. Some form of this principle is taught in many religious cultures, but here's the twist: when I give someone something, I'm not saying that person gives me something back – that almost never happens. Way more than 90% of the time they don't even appreciate it. Instead, overall, gifts in life come in from all different ways. It's not just financial gifts, it's emotional, health, everything.

My faith was fueled by the underlying goodness in my parents. This book is dedicated to my mom and dad who gave me more than I can ever repay. Up until now, they are the only ones. For everyone else, I have a fanatical desire to out-give them and, so far, I'm winning.

Monitor Results in Giving

Like other areas of my life and business, I also monitor results in giving. I do what works. When I started becoming wealthy, I did my homework. In charity, you can give a lot of money to different groups and different places and be no one, or you can focus on something and make a lasting difference. The more I learned, the more I felt compelled to end world hunger. Every 3.6 seconds someone dies from hunger. One in six people do not get enough food to be healthy and lead an active life, making hunger and malnutrition the number one health risk worldwide. Tonight, almost one billion people will go to bed hungry.[10]

There's a difference between malnutrition (when an individual fails to meet the minimum intake of calories) and starvation. Prolonged starvation can cause permanent organ damage and lead to death. Here's the heart-breaking reality - the world produces enough food for everyone, so it's just a transportation problem. Exacerbating this issue, the great majority of hunger deaths do not come from starvation but from nutrition-related sicknesses and diseases. In this century, with all of our technological advances and entrepreneurial knowledge, there is no reason for anyone to die of hunger or hunger-related diseases.

In keeping my promise to God, I began investigating different world hunger organizations. We met with groups from Phoenix to Washington D.C., beating the bushes looking for some organization that shared my goal of stopping hunger today. We couldn't find one. While many of them are doing great work, none seemed like the right fit. They were feeding the hungry, but they were also doing an additional thing: proselytizing (sharing their religious beliefs) or producing income. I do feel these goals are worthwhile. It's important to tell those in need about God or to teach self-sufficiency through farming, fishing or manufacturing. I just don't feel called to help with these additional goals. I just want to save lives and keep the focus on feeding. People keep dying of hunger.

We finally resorted to doing it ourselves. In 1989, we began The Hewitt Foundation to fight hunger and save lives. Again, we wanted to set the standard and improve each day with the fanatical goal of SOLVING world hunger. We feel like the Marines, we're the first one to arrive there, feed the hungry, and then turn them over to the Army or Navy to take charge. Then we want to go to the next beachhead.

Set Unrealistic Goals

Some people would say that's crazy, just like the decision to take on H&R Block in 1982. It's crazy like the decision in 1997, when I started competing against the company that bore my own name, Jackson Hewitt, expecting to be number one in the universe. People would say these are unrealistic goals, so why not add another? The bottom line is that no one has solved world hunger yet.

Coincidentally, during the time I was researching global malnutrition and hunger, our family attended a Methodist Church. Our minister introduced us to two other ministers who had started an organization called the Society of Saint Andrew, in the Western part of Virginia. They had been running this group for about 14 years and my oldest daughter, Patti, had gone "gleaning" with them. With certain harvests, especially potatoes and apples, farmers have machines that do the harvesting, but they aren't efficient enough to catch 100% of the fruit. There is usually 5-10% remaining in the fields, so this ministry bussed in middle school and high school kids who go out and pick up the leftovers, put them into bushels, and send them to Appalachia, a very poor region.

Take a Step to Begin

Every once in a while The Society of Saint Andrew would get a request to help overseas. They would call me up or come and see me and say, "I have this project in Ethiopia and I need $17,000. The food is free if you'll provide the shipping." I'd write a check and send it off. This went on for about four to five years.

In 1997, Ray Buchanan, one of the two founders of that organization, came in for another project: $30,000 for rice to South Korea. We had a conversation that led to the founding of another organization. In meeting for lunch, I asked how he was doing. He said, "Oh, woe is me (I may be paraphrasing here). I went to Africa for two weeks and saw all of these people starving to death." He said, "I have to go there and help. I have to change – I just can't stand by and do nothing." I asked him, "If you had a dream and could do anything you wanted, what would it be?" He said, "I would go to places where disasters occurred, I'd come back and within two weeks, I would send food." I said, "Well, my dream is almost the same. Except, I would want you to have a phone and start sending the food right away, when you are there." The same

month we opened Liberty Tax Service, in January of 1998, Ray Buchanan and I founded *Stop Hunger Now*. As of this writing, Stop Hunger Now has sent more than 158 million meals to 65 countries. In 2013, Community Relations Manager, Lee Warren wrote me a touching letter of thanks.

November 19, 2013
Dear John,

I joined Stop Hunger Now in 2006 to take the program into Virginia, yet we never had the opportunity to get to know each other. To get to the point immediately, I'm at the age in life where expressing gratitude is something I take more seriously than ever. When someone comes to mind, I make a point to contact them.

This past weekend during a long trail run, I was going over in my head a presentation I am to give in Pennsylvania this week about SHN. Since I always recount your contribution to co-founding SHN in my speeches, you came to mind, but in my solitude, with no distractions, I stopped my speech rehearsal and began to focus in on the gratitude I have for all that you allowed us to create.

Over 122 million meals in just about 8 years! As Ray Buchanan and our team were headed to the Philippines to work with our partners, not just to distribute the meals already on the water, but to set up an SHN packaging event (through Rotary) so Filipinos can help their own right in their own country, I was once again in awe of the power of one person, with a vision, to change the world. Then one person became two people and now hundreds of thousands of people around the world know the privilege of contributing to the alleviation of hunger.

Thank you. Sincerely, thank you. You and Ray gave me the opportunity to live out a God-given purpose and you gave all of us a channel for good.

Sincerely,
Lee
Lee Warren
Community Relations Manager - Stop Hunger Now

Keep Your Laser Focus

As the years progressed, Ray's focus for *Stop Hunger Now* turned to sharing his religion, but my dream never changed – to SOLVE world hunger.

In 2011, my associate, Chuck Lovelace, and I took our investigation of world hunger to a new level. One of the problems with most of the food organizations I've seen is that they are focusing on so many countries that nothing gets solved. Where are the results? I believe we have to have a laser focus and solve this in one place at a time. We came up with an idea of Run for Food International, with the goal of SOLVING the hunger crisis in one country. If we can end hunger in one place, then from there we will learn and keep building on that. We decided to test this in two to four countries, monitor results, and apply our findings to other countries. We have started partnering with other groups, creating innovative and sustainable solutions to save lives and end hunger, once and for all. One place at a time. This is a strategy no one else is trying.

Do Extensive Homework

After extensive research, we chose Nicaragua as one of our first test countries. It is classified by the World Bank as the second poorest country in Latin America and the Caribbean. According to a statement from the National Survey of Demographic and Health, 23% of children there under the age of five suffer from chronic under-nutrition. Once a prosperous nation, this country fell prey to recurrent natural disasters, such as droughts, hurricanes, floods and earthquakes along with political pressures. Extreme poverty shapes food consumption patterns and many Nicaraguan families have reduced their meat and dairy consumption, invested less on health and education and, in some cases, removed their children from school. World Food Programme studies have shown that stunting among children under the age of 3 in WFP targeted areas is higher than the national average, estimated at 30%.[11]

In 2013, we visited the Nicaraguan Embassy in Washington D.C. The diplomats asked us, "What are you going to do?" I answered, "Well, we're just going to try everything we can think of. No one has ever solved it." Our focus is on results. We will set the standard and improve each day.

To Whom Much is Given, Much is Required

While our hunger solution project is just beginning, today my legacy is changing thousands of people's lives through business. That's my reward. In creating the culture of Liberty, we received another gift that I never expected. For some

reason, Liberty Tax attracts people who are committed to changing lives in their own ways, through many great causes. These partners and employees come to the table with generosity in their hearts. I can't claim any credit for their compassionate spirits; this is simply a family that already has giving at its core. The Fortunate Must Give Back isn't a principle I have to teach; it is organically part of our culture, including feeding the hungry in our local communities.

HOW DID YOU KNOW THAT WE HAD NO FOOD?
By Sheryl Romaniuk/Zee - Washington State

The most impoverished zip code in the entire state of Washington is located in our territory. Nearly three-quarters of students at the public schools around us qualify for free or reduced lunch. The need surrounding us is great.

On December 21st, our store gave a complete turkey dinner to 100 of our neediest local families. The dinner included a 14 lb turkey, canned sides, a bag of potatoes, rolls and a pumpkin pie. Families were identified by guidance counselors at four local elementary schools. From the employees who volunteered their time, to local businesses who donated sides at reduced costs, to the service group from a nearby university who helped us prep for the big day, the turnout and support we received was remarkable. Even our local news station showed up! Nearly all the turkey dinners were picked up by the families or delivered to their homes by our volunteers.

There were a few families who did not come and whom we could not contact so these extra dinners were delivered to clients in the neighborhood. One of these clients lives just down the street from our office. When she opened her door to find our manager standing there with a box of food, she burst into tears. "How did you know?" she cried, "How did you know that we had no food?"

We hope to continue growing our partnership with local businesses so that next year, we can increase the number of Christmas meals provided to 200. We see a lot of need in our community, and though it is easy to become overwhelmed by that need, there is comfort in knowing that in a small way, we are making a difference.

Find Your Giving Passion

Fighting hunger is just one way our Liberty family is transforming communities. We have employees who devote much of their time to the fight against cancer, muscular dystrophy, local blood drives, improving the lives of children and the list goes on. In our culture book and blog, *Fanatical at Liberty*, our franchisees and employees tell their stories of changing lives in their own neighborhoods, like Felicia Bowden who began by reaching out to just one person.

HIRING THE HOMELESS
By Felicia Bowden/Zee & Area Developer - Evansville, IN
Fanatical Award Winner for David!

Three years ago I had a waver, David Hensler, who was just awesome. He was the best I'd seen: hardworking, honest, strong faith, and clean - but homeless much of the time. He left the area after that tax season, but the next year I got him a job in Colorado, and last year he worked for a Zee in Corpus Christi.

I was friends with him on Facebook and I would always ask him to come back. This year, I did the same and it just so happened that he was out of work, out of money, out of food, and his wife had just left him. I sent him a bus ticket and $70 - enough to get food for a week and minutes on his phone.

When he arrived, I had warm clothes for him and he had made arrangements to stay at the Evansville Rescue Mission - where he had stayed before. I took him to get food (he hadn't eaten in 2 days) and took him to my main office to store his "stuff" so it wouldn't get stolen at the shelter.

I took him to the Mission that night and they wouldn't let him in because he wasn't going to be in Evansville permanently. I got him dinner and took him to one of my other new offices where he stayed the night and painted for me. Within a couple of days he got into the Mission.

On Christmas Eve, when it was 21 degrees, the Mission kicked him out and put him back on the street. He went to the United Caring Shelter in Evansville where he has been staying since. One of my other wavers who "came with the store" when I bought it has also been helping him - she had him over for Christmas and lets him do his laundry.

He has been working hard for us, waving and increasing visibility. He also is recruiting wavers for us at the shelters. He has the best attitude and is always "blessed" when you ask how he is. He was featured in the *Evansville Courier and Press,* the local newspaper, and told the reporter how great the people at Liberty are hiring the homeless and taking care of them.

- Posted on www.fanaticalatliberty.com

Yes, my goals are huge, audacious and unrealistic. For my business, my purpose is to win as a fanatical entrepreneur, to be number one in the universe or die trying. For my kids, it's most important for me to set a good example and introduce them to God. For you, it's been my job to challenge and, hopefully, annoy you out of your comfort zone. In your game of life and business, will you choose to be a winner or a loser? Just normal or beyond extraordinary?

So here is my final challenge for you: whose life will you change, starting with just ONE person? Integrity means being committed to do what you say you're going to do. How will you compete to win your game? No matter what you are doing, act like an owner and never quit. Keep persevering and, in my book, you can also call yourself a winner.

JOHN'S PRINCIPLES TO LIVE BY

- The fortunate must give back
- What's your deal with God?
- Monitor results in giving
- Set unrealistic goals
- Take a step to begin
- Keep your laser focus
- Do extensive homework
- To whom much is given, much is required
- Find your giving passion

Your Challenge

Whose life will you change, starting with just ONE person?

Our Mission

Set the standard, improve each day and have some fun!

Our Principles

- Create raving fans!
- Be honest, show respect and have integrity
- Monitor results, not activities
- Mistakes are a wise person's education
- Challenge ourselves, challenge each other, break boundaries
- Give loyalty - Get loyalty
- Communication, Communication, Communication
- Attitude is a matter of choice - you make the right choice
- Enjoy the journey - do it with pride
- Contribute to the team

Notes

(Endnotes)

1 Crosby, Kathy Lee. "Let the Magic Begin," Simon & Schuster, 1997, pgs 18-19.

2 Family of Vince Lombardi c/o Luminary Group LLC, "Famous Quotes by Vince Lombardi," http://www.vincelombardi.com/quotes.html.

3 Jack Welch, "GE 2000 Annual Report," http://www.rightattitudes.com/2008/02/06/jack-welch-four-types-of-managers/

4 "This Day in History" 7/23/1885, http://www.history.com/this-day-in-history/former-president-ulysses-s-grant-dies

5 NationsBank was one of the largest banking corporations in the United States, based in Charlotte, North Carolina. In 1998, it acquired BankAmerica to become Bank of America. http://en.wikipedia.org/wiki/NationsBank

6 http://www.forbes.com/sites/keldjensen/2012/08/08/rock-bottom-how-great-leaders-triumph-over-failure/

7. http://business.time.com/2012/02/16/top-9-celebrity-bankruptcies/slide/walt-disney-3/ and http://bankruptcy.uslegal.com/profilesfamousbankruptcies/walt-disney/

8 http://www.forbes.com/sites/nathanfurr/2011/06/09/how-failure-taught-edison-to-repeatedly-innovate/

9 http://inventors.about.com/library/lessons/bl_appendix5.htm and http://en.wikipedia.org/wiki/Charles_Holland_Duell

10 https://www.runforfoodinternational.org/faq.php

11 http://www.wfp.org/countries/nicaragua/overview

John's Suggested Reading List and Other Sources Consulted

Peter F. Drucker, *The Effective Executive: The Definitive Guide to Getting the Right Things Done* (HarperBusiness; Revised edition, 2006).

Seth Godin, *The Dip: A Little Book that Teaches You When to Quit (and When to Stick)* (Portfolio Hardcover, 2007).

Seth Godin, *Small is the New Big: and 183 Other Riffs, Rants, and Remarkable Business Ideas* (Portfolio Hardcover, 2006).

Seth Godin, *Purple Cow: Transform Your Business by Being Remarkable* (Portfolio, 2003)

Stan Phelps, *What's Your Purple Goldfish: How to Win Customers & Influence Word of Mouth* (9 INCH Marketing, 2012).

John C. Maxwell and Steven R. Covey, *The 21 Irrefutable Laws of Leadership: Follow Them and People will Follow You* (Thomas Nelson; Revised & Updated edition, 2007).

John C. Maxwell, *The Difference Maker: Making Your Attitude Your Greatest Asset* (Thomas Nelson, 2006).

Dave Logan, John King, Halee Fischer-Wright and Halee Fischer-Wright, *Tribal Leadership: Leveraging Natural Groups to Build a Thriving Organization* (HarperBusiness; Reprint edition, 2011).

Ton Hsieh, *Delivering Happiness: A Path to Profits, Passion, and Purpose* (Business Plus; Reprint edition, 2013).

Dale Carnegie, *How to Stop Worrying and Start Living: Time-Tested Methods for Conquering Worry* (Pocket Books; Revised edition, 1990).

Dale Carnegie, *How to Win Friends and Influence People* (Pocket Books, 1998).

Malcolm Gladwell, *Outliers: The Story of Success* (Back Bay Books; Reprint edition, 2011).

Malcolm Gladwell, *Blink: The Power of Thinking Without Thinking* (Back Bay Books, 2007)

Kevin Maney, *Trade-Off: Why Some Things Catch on and Others Don't* (Crown Business, 2010).

Al Ries and Jack Trout, *The 22 Immutable Laws of Marketing: Violate Them at Your Own Risk* (HarperBusiness, 1994).

Thomas B. Smith, Michael A Markowski, and Marjorie L. Markowski, *If It Is To Be, It's Up to Me: How to Develop the Attitude of a Winner and Become a Leader* (Possibility Press; 2nd edition, 2014).

Robert T. Kiyosaki, with Sharon L. Lechter, *Rich Dad, Poor Dad: What the Rich Teach Their Kids About Money - That the Poor and Middle Class Do Not!* (Warner Business Books, 2000).

Robert T. Kiyosaki, *Rich Dad's Cashflow Quadrant: Rich Dad's Guide to Financial Freedom* (Plata Publishing, 2011).

Mark Sanborn, *The Fred Factor: How Passion in Your Work and Life Can Turn the Ordinary into the Extraordinary* (Currency, 2004).

Terry R. Bacon, *What People Want: A Manager's Guide to Building Relationships that Work* (Nicholas Brealey America, 2011).

Joe Mathews, Don DeBolt and Deb Percival, *Street Smart Franchising* (Entrepreneur, 2006).

Dave Anderson, *If You Don't Make Waves You'll Drown: 10 Hard Charging Strategies for Leading in Politically Correct Times* (John Wiley & Sons, Inc., 2005).

Stephanie Winston, *The Organized Executive: The Classic Program for Productivity: New Ways to Manage Time, Paper, People, and the Digital Office* (Business Plus, 2001)

Kenneth H. Blanchard and Spencer Johnson, *The One Minute Manager* (William Morrow, 2003)

Kenneth H. Blanchard, William Oncken, Jr. and Hal Burrows, *One Minute Manager Meets the Monkey* (Quill, 1991)

Michael E. Gerber, *The E-Myth Revisited: Why Most Small Businesses Don't Work and What to Do About It* (HarperCollins, 2004)

Harry Beckwith, *Selling the Invisible: A Field Guide to Modern Marketing* (Business Plus, 2012)

Sam Walton with John Huey, *Sam Walton: Made in America: My Story* (Bantam, 1993)

Kevin Freiberg and Jackie Freiberg, *Nuts! Southwest Airlines' Crazy Recipes for Business and Personal Success* (Crown Business, 1998)

Jon Spoelstra, *Marketing Outrageously: How to Increase Your Revenue by Staggering Amounts* (Bard Press, 2001)

Jay Conrad Levinson, *Guerrilla Marketing: Secrets for Making Big Profits from Your Small Business* (Houghton Mifflin Company, 1998)

Stephen C. Lundin, John Christensen and Harry Paul, *Fish! A Remarkable Way to Boost Morale and Improve Results* (Hyperion, 2000)

Shawn Doyle, *10 Foundations of Motivation: How to Get Motivated and Stay Motivated* (iUniverse, Inc., 2003)

James Collins, *Built to Last: Successful Habits of Visionary Companies* (HarperBusiness, 2004)

a Book's Mind

Whether you want to purchase bulk copies of
iCompete
or buy another book for a friend, get it now at:
www.abooksmart.com

If you have a book that you would like to publish,
contact Floyd Orfield, Publisher, at A Book's Mind:
floyd@abooksmind.com.

www.abooksmind.com